Walks along
the Thames Path

Walks along the Thames Path

RON EMMONS

25 CIRCULAR WALKS FROM
THAMES HEAD TO GREENWICH

TED SMART

This edition produced for
The Book People Ltd
Hall Wood Avenue
Haydock
St Helens WA11 9UL

First published in 2001 by
New Holland Publishers (UK) Ltd
www.newhollandpublishers.com
London • Cape Town • Sydney • Auckland

ISBN 1 84330 077 X

Publishing Manager: Jo Hemmings
Project Editor: Michaella Standen
Copy Editor: Gill Harvey
Packagers: Hardlines, Charlbury

Reproduction by Pica Colour Separation Overseas (Pte) Ltd, Singapore
Printed and bound in Singapore by Kyodo Printing Co (Singapore) Pte Ltd

Photographic Acknowledgements
All photographs by the author with the exception of the following:
David Paterson: Plates 31, 32, 33

Front cover: View across the Thames to Windsor Castle from the Brocas in Eton
Back cover: The River Leach as it passes under a house in Lechlade before joining
the Thames
Spine: Statue of Father Thames at St John's Lock, Lechlade
Cover photographs by Ron Emmons.

Contents

Preface

I was born on the banks of the River Thames, and its restless spirit must have affected me because as soon as I could, I began to travel. As a result, I have stood beside several of the world's mightiest rivers – the Nile, the Amazon, the Yangtze and the Colorado. As years went on, however, I began to wonder about the island of my birth, of which I knew so little. I felt that the best way to get to know the country was to walk beside the Thames from beginning to end, paying close attention to nature, the buildings and local people. So I walked the river twice, in the summers of 1998 and 1999, the second time to research this book; and I now feel a familiarity with the ancient and complex culture of England.

I owe thanks to many people for the realization of this project. First to Jo Hemmings of New Holland, who saw its potential, and to Michaella Standen for helping to give it shape. Next to all those who helped me out with useful information or comments – Jos Joslin, National Trails Officer; Ann and David Beasley, Charles Westmore, Leslie Drain, Longshanks and Talesman, who shared their knowledge on guided walks. Also to countless unnamed people who answered my phone queries about opening times and other details. Last, but not least, thanks to Mum and Dad for their invaluable support.

Comments on any aspects of these walks are most welcome and should be addressed to ronemmon@hotmail.com

Key to Route Maps

Each of the walks in this book is accompanied by a map on which the route of the walk is shown in blue. Places of interest – such as historic buildings, museums and churches – are clearly identified. Addresses, telephone numbers and e-mail addresses for public attractions are given in the Further Information Section on page 150.

route of main walk	APP	Approach	N	North
route of Thames Path	ARC	Arcade	PH	Public House (Pub)
access to public transport/car park	AVE	Avenue	PK	Park
route of river/canal	BR	Bridge	PL	Place
railway line	CL	Close	R	River
major buildings	CRES	Crescent	RD	Road
church	CT	Court	S	South
public toilets	DR	Drive	ST	Saint
parks	E	East	ST	Street
information	GDNS	Gardens	TER	Terrace
Underground	HO	House	WK	Walk
Docklands Light Railway	LA	Lane	W	West
rail station				

Introduction

The River Thames is, in many ways, the lifeblood of England. It has given birth to many of the country's vital communities, such as Oxford, Windsor and, of course, London. Until recently, the river was used mainly by pleasure boaters, who chugged up and down its length in cruisers and narrow boats. Then, in 1996, the Thames Path was inaugurated as a National Trail, and now anyone with two working legs and a pair of shoes can walk the entire length of the river. However, this takes a couple of weeks or more, and the walks in this book have been compiled for those who would prefer to let the river unravel its secrets gradually.

The Thames Path stretches for 294 kilometres (183 miles), beginning beside a rough stone marker in a Gloucestershire field and ending at the gleaming cowls of the Thames Barrier, to the east of London. The walks in this book explore the countryside and towns in between, and are organized in order, from the source to the Barrier. The locations have been chosen to give a variety of mood and interest; some focus more on the natural surroundings while others are rich in history. Where there are nearby places of special interest, these are included as options. Of course, you may approach the walks in any order you choose, but you will gain a better understanding of the river's character if you follow it from infant gurglings to maturity. Where possible, the walks have been planned to go with the flow of the river, i.e. downstream.

Each walk begins with a quick summary to give you the flavour of the area. This is followed by logistics (starting point, length of walk, refreshment options, etc.), then by any relevant background information and a description of the walk itself. Here are a few general words about logistics:

Start/Finish: Where possible, walks start at a convenient point for both car parking and public transport, though in some cases walkers arriving by public transport join the walk part-way through. Grid references (GR) are given for the start of each. The first three numbers give the horizontal location, and the last three give the vertical location. Ordnance Survey Maps for each walk are as follows:

Walk		Walk		Walk	
1	Explorer 168 & 169	10	Explorer 170	18	Explorer 160
2	Explorer 169	11	Explorer 170	19	Explorer 160
3	Explorer 169	12	Explorer 170	20	Explorer 160
4	Explorer 170	13	Explorer 171	21	Explorer 161
5	Explorer 170	14	Explorer 171	22	Explorer 161
6	Explorer 180	15	Explorer 171	23	Explorer 161
7	Explorer 180	16	Explorer 172	24	Explorer 173
8	Explorer 180 & 170	17	Explorer 172	25	Explorer 161
9	Explorer 170				

Access: Instructions on how to get to the start of each walk are given for both private and public transport users. The Thames Path is particularly well served by trains and buses, apart from remote areas near the source, where services are infrequent. For detailed information, consult the relevant train or bus authorities listed at the back of the book. Do not forget that boat services operate on some sections, offering another way to experience the river and its moods.

Length and Time: The walks range from 5.5 kilometres (3½ miles) to 15 kilometres (9¼ miles) and are intended to stretch your legs rather than present you with any great challenge. Most of the walks are on flat ground, though a few involve a little climbing, and most can be easily covered in half a day. This allows the rest of the day for travelling and/or exploring nearby towns and villages. It would also be quite possible to cover two nearby walks in a day. Times are calculated at a steady stroll, so if you are a particularly fast or slow walker, revise them accordingly.

Refreshments: Almost all the walks pass pubs, tea houses or restaurants, many of which are full of character and offer a welcome break. Keep in mind that most country pubs close between 15.00 and 18.00. Alternatively, you might like to take a packed lunch and enjoy it along the way.

Opening Times: These can change at short notice, so it's a good idea to call and check them before setting out. Unfortunately, admission charges are even more prone to fluctuation, so specifics are not given.

Clothing: Comfortable walking shoes are recommended for all walks, though trainers may be sufficient in London. After heavy rain, wellingtons or galoshes are a good idea on walks near the source (numbers 1–6). Long trousers are preferable to shorts, as some areas can get overgrown with nettles and brambles. As the British climate is so unpredictable, always take waterproofs with you.

When to Walk: Each season has its charm. Winter walking offers the chance to get away from it all, but bear in mind that the path may be slippery, particularly in the upper reaches, and that many attractions are closed from October to March. In general, the best weather for walking occurs between April and September.

How to Walk: There are some basic courtesies that you should always observe when walking, to ensure that you leave the locals and the environment unharmed by your visit. These are:
• leave no litter along the way
• close gates behind you
• resist any temptation to stray from the official path
• walk on the right along country lanes that have no pavements
• keep dogs on leads where crossing fields with animals

Finally, a summary of the benefits of walking the Thames Path: walking tones up your body, and gazing at nature soothes the mind. Being beside rivers refreshes the spirit, and visiting historic monuments expands your cultural knowledge. If you remain aware of your body movements as you walk, you can also practise meditation.

Historical Background

Long ago, before Britain was separated from continental Europe, the Thames was a tributary of the Rhine, which flowed into the North Sea. The English Channel was formed about 7,000 years ago at the end of the last Ice Age, along with the enormous estuary that gives the southeast coast of England its distinctive shape. When invaders came – the Romans, the Danes and later the French – they all used the river to penetrate deep into England and subdue its people.

William the Conqueror, who arrived in 1066, understood that a river has two vital characteristics – it can act as a highway, and as a barrier. To secure his new kingdom, he built castles along the banks of the Thames at places like Windsor. Soon, great abbeys and monasteries were also erected on its banks, and by the late 13th century the river was used to carry wool, which had become the country's main product. It is no coincidence that the Magna Carta, now seen as the foundation of democracy, was signed by King John in 1215 on the banks of the Thames; nor is it a surprise that its key clauses, relating to basic human rights, are intermingled with others relating to its weirs and navigation. At that time, whoever exerted control over the river also had power over the whole country.

When the age of world exploration got under way, the Thames provided a safe harbour for returning boats laden with exotic goods, and was therefore of vital importance in the growth of the British Empire. In the late 18th and early 19th centuries, newly built canals linked the river to waterways nationwide; and a system of towpaths was constructed along its banks to enable barges laden with coal and stone, cheese and cloth to navigate its length. These towpaths stretched from Lechlade to Putney in London, and switched from bank to bank to avoid weak verges or private land. The crossings were linked by ferries that carried both horses and halers (human barge pullers).

Successive sovereigns followed in William's footsteps, building riverside palaces at Hampton, Richmond, and Greenwich. Elizabeth I was so enamoured of the river that in 1592 she visited the remote source to look at 'the very first trickle of my fine Thames'.

The Empire, along with the barges, is now long gone. The coming of railways and roads made river transport seem slow and therefore expensive; and the towpaths were reclaimed by nature, becoming overgrown with shrubs and wild flowers. However, without these towpaths, there would be no Thames Path. As far back as the 1930s, the idea of restoring them for recreational use was proposed by local councils. Their calls were later echoed by the River Thames Society and the Ramblers' Association; but it was not until the 1980s, when the Countryside Commission declared the project feasible, that work went ahead. Three new footbridges were built, the towpath was repaired in many places, over 1,200 signposts were erected, and hundreds of stiles were installed or repaired. The result is that, apart from a few minor detours, it is now possible to walk beside the river from start to finish. These 25 circular walks take you to the most attractive and interesting sections of that riparian path.

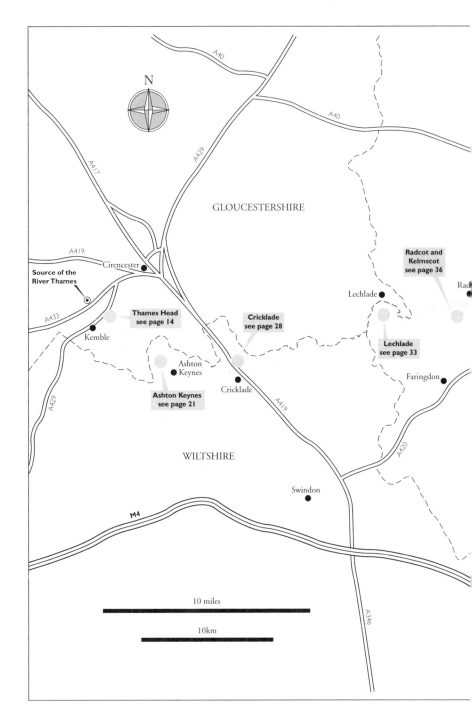

N

GLOUCESTERSHIRE

Radcot and
Kelmscot
see page 36

Rad

A419

Source of the
River Thames

Cirencester

Lechlade

Thames Head
see page 14

Cricklade
see page 28

Lechlade
see page 33

Kemble

Ashton
Keynes

Faringdon

Ashton Keynes
see page 21

Cricklade

WILTSHIRE

Swindon

M4

10 miles

10km

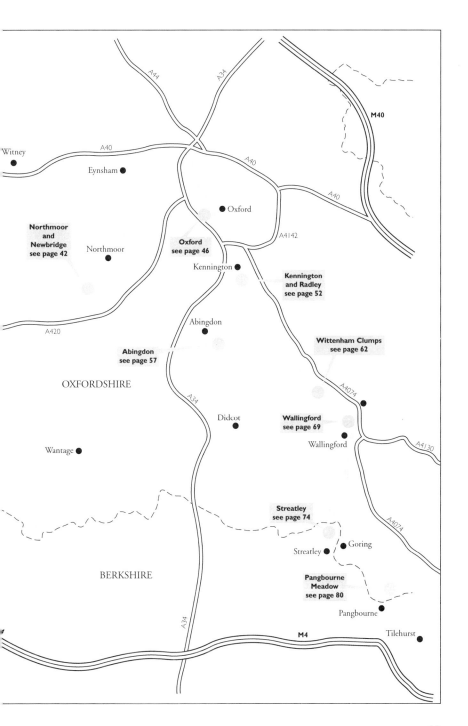

Witney

A44

A34

A40

Eynsham

M40

Oxford

A40

A40

Northmoor and Newbridge see page 42

Northmoor

Oxford see page 46

A4142

Kennington

Kennington and Radley see page 52

Abingdon

A420

Wittenham Clumps see page 62

Abingdon see page 57

OXFORDSHIRE

A34

A4074

Didcot

Wallingford see page 69

Wallingford

A4130

Wantage

A4074

Streatley see page 74

Streatley   Goring

BERKSHIRE

Pangbourne Meadow see page 80

A34

Pangbourne

M4

Tilehurst

11

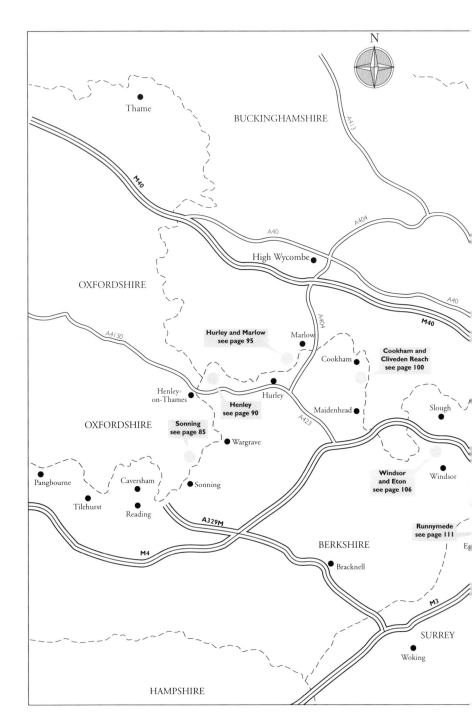

N

Thame

BUCKINGHAMSHIRE

A413

M40

A404

A40

High Wycombe

OXFORDSHIRE

A40

M40

A4130

A404

Hurley and Marlow see page 95

Marlow

Cookham

Cookham and Cliveden Reach see page 100

Henley-on-Thames

Hurley

Henley see page 90

Maidenhead

A423

Slough

OXFORDSHIRE

Sonning see page 85

Wargrave

Windsor

Pangbourne

Caversham

Sonning

Windsor and Eton see page 106

Windsor

Tilehurst

Reading

A329M

Runnymede see page 111

BERKSHIRE

Eg

M4

Bracknell

M3

SURREY

Woking

HAMPSHIRE

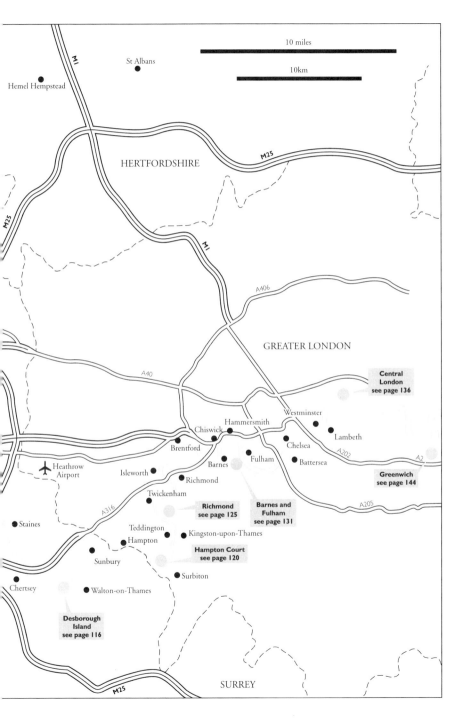

10 miles

10km

St Albans

Hemel Hempstead

M1

M25

HERTFORDSHIRE

M25

M1

A406

GREATER LONDON

A40

Central London
see page 136

Westminster

Chiswick

Hammersmith

Lambeth

Brentford

Chelsea

A202

A2

Heathrow Airport

Barnes

Fulham

Battersea

Isleworth

Greenwich
see page 144

Richmond

Twickenham

A316

A205

Richmond
see page 125

Barnes and Fulham
see page 131

Staines

Teddington

Kingston-upon-Thames

Hampton

Hampton Court
see page 120

Sunbury

Surbiton

Chertsey

Walton-on-Thames

Desborough Island
see page 116

M25

SURREY

Thames Head

Summary: This walk begins by taking you across a couple of fields right to the official source of the Thames. This is usually dry, but as the route passes south through fields, there is evidence of its presence before Lyd Well, where it often appears for the first time. After passing the outskirts of Kemble village, the path follows the tiny stream as it bends towards the east and the village of Ewen. The return is along quiet country roads, then across fields and past the disused Thames & Severn Canal, and thus back to the source.

Location:	152 kilometres (95 miles) west of London; 64 kilometres (40 miles) west of Oxford.
Visitor attractions:	Official source of the Thames; Lyd Well; village of Ewen; disused Thames & Severn Canal.
Start/Finish:	Northwest side of railway bridge over A433 (Fosse Way), 5 kilometres (3 miles) southwest of Cirencester. OS Explorer map 168, GR 982987.
Access:	(*by car*) Head from Cirencester towards Tetbury on the A433. After about 5 kilometres (3 miles), turn right immediately after you go under a railway bridge and park.
	(*by train*) Take a train from Paddington via Swindon to Kemble. Walk down the approach to the station and turn left on the road leading to Tarlton. Go under a railway bridge and up to the junction with the A433. Turn right, pass the Thames Head Inn on the left, and then turn left just before the railway bridge ahead.
Length:	10.5 kilometres (6½ miles).
Time:	3 hours.
Refreshments:	Thames Head Inn (100 metres west of starting point on A433); Wild Duck Inn (Ewen); Tunnel House Inn (Sapperton Tunnel).
Pathway status:	Country paths; dirt tracks; sealed roads.
Best time to visit:	The best time to visit the source is after heavy rain, when it begins higher. The channel is usually dry in summer.

Background

There are those who argue, quite understandably, that the true source of the Thames is at Seven Springs, which lies 5 kilometres (3 miles) south of Cheltenham, just west of the junction of the A435 and A436 roads. This spring is 210 metres (700 feet) above sea level, compared with 107 metres (356 feet) at Thames Head, and is 24 kilometres (15 miles) further from the sea. There is also a Latin inscription here, stating that this is the sevenfold fount of the Thames. However, the stream that runs from here to Cricklade has always been known as the Churn.

The official source at Thames Head often disappoints visitors as it is usually dry, but if you are patient, and not walking after a long dry spell, you will probably encounter the river's first gurglings somewhere along this route. Its first waters frequently arise at Lyd Well, which sits in a glade about 1.5 kilometres (1 mile) below Thames Head. This is believed to have been built by the Romans, who also established nearby Corinium (now known as Cirencester), the second-largest town in the country at the time. A walk around this classic Cotswold town, particularly its well laid-out museum, is an ideal complement to this initial ramble by the river.

As well as reminding us of England's Roman history, this walk shows the importance of transport by water before the age of railways and good roads. The Thames & Severn Canal, which you will pass towards the end, was one of the greatest engineering projects of its day when it was built in the late 18th century.

The Walk

Seeking the Source
Walk up the shady pathway to the left of the railway track, which leads out on to a former railway siding. Abandoned tankers stand forlorn, and wild flowers sprout from between half-buried concrete slabs and railway sleepers. Go ahead beyond the siding to a stile, cross the railway line with care (this is not a disused line!), then climb the concrete stile on the opposite side. If you look ahead into the valley from here, you will see a grassy path that leads diagonally left down a slope towards a dense copse of trees. Just in front of this copse, the Thames has its humble origins.

Walk down the path, cross a stile and walk along the left of a field beside a dry-stone wall. Beautifully crafted walls such as this are a major feature of the Cotswold countryside, and are rarely seen further downstream. This walk, however, allows plenty of opportunity to appreciate them. As you approach the end of the field, branch right to a gate and cross the stile next to it. Walk towards the copse, and as you near it you will notice a stone slab to the left of a large ash tree. In front of the slab is a depression in the ground, usually filled with stones. You are looking at the official source of the Thames, as decided by the Conservators of the River Thames in 1958, on the occasion of their centenary. A statue of Father Thames reclined here from 1958 to 1974, but was removed to St John's Lock at Lechlade (see page 36) to protect him from vandals.

Don't be disappointed at the lack of water. With luck, on the day of your visit, you will have found where the river chooses to rise before you complete this walk. Retrace your steps as far as the last stile and, instead of branching right back towards the railway, go straight ahead to another stile, where a signpost indicates the Thames Path. From here, the route goes south in search of the River Thames.

The Magic of Lyd Well
Follow the path along the right-hand side of a field, which has a couple of lonely cottages standing in its far left-hand corner. At the end of this field, the route takes you over a stile by a barred gate, and brings you out on Fosse Way (A433). Just 20

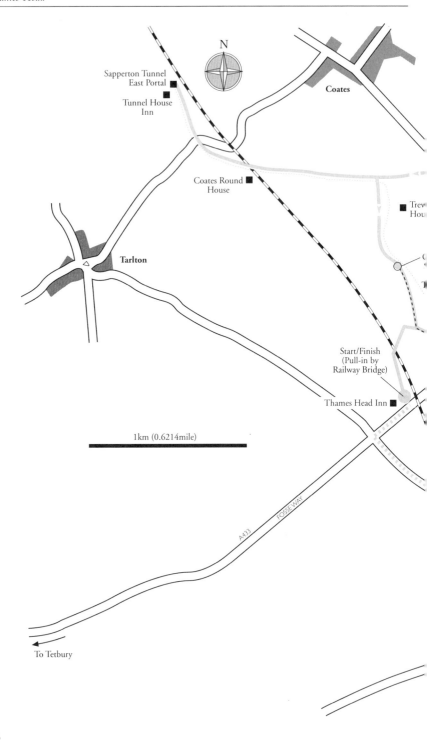

Sapperton Tunnel
East Portal

Tunnel House
Inn

Coates

Coates Round
House

Trev
Hou

Tarlton

N

Start/Finish
(Pull-in by
Railway Bridge)

Thames Head Inn

1km (0.6214mile)

A433

FOSSE WAY

To Tetbury

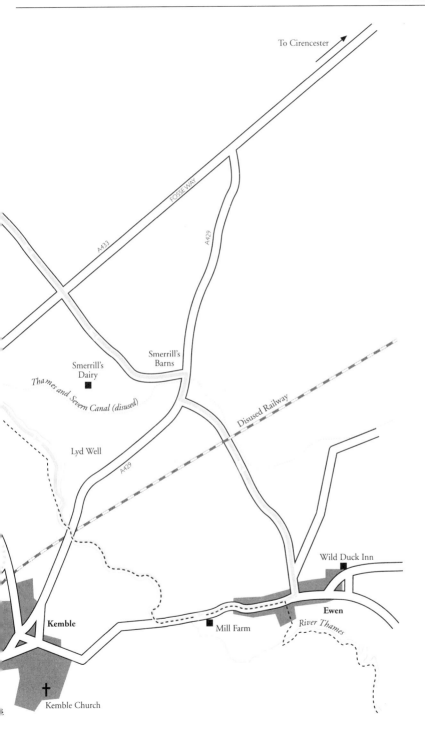

To Cirencester

FOSSE WAY

A433

A429

Smerrill's
Barns

Smerrill's
Dairy

Thames and Severn Canal (disused)

Lyd Well

A429

Disused Railway

Wild Duck Inn

Kemble

Mill Farm

Ewen

River Thames

✝ Kemble Church

metres (22 yards) to the left of the gate, a tiny culvert in the undergrowth is the first technical bridging point of the Thames. Cross the busy road with care, and then go over another stile leading into a long field. The path may not be very clear, but you need to head towards the distant spire of Kemble church. As you approach the middle of the field, look at the lowest lying area, which runs in front of a line of hawthorns. Even if there is no water, you can make out the beginnings of a channel with low banks, snaking across the left of the field. Just as the last walk of this book (Greenwich) offers the sole opportunity to walk under the river, you now have a rare chance to walk along the riverbed.

Leave the field by a stile in its right-hand corner, then go left to a dell at the beginning of the next field. To the right of this dell is a low dry-stone wall, from which the nascent Thames may be emerging. To look at Lyd Well, go round to the left of the fenced-off dell. After heavy rain, clear water surges from the well, then spirals round and down to join the main channel of the river, making this dell a magical place. Whether there is water or not, the channel is obvious from here on; the grass lies flat on the riverbed, showing the direction of the river's flow. It is also thick with water crowfoot and other delicate flowers, and its far bank is lined with willows.

As you follow the channel towards the end of the field, you may become aware of traffic on the A429, which the route will cross shortly. The banks here are more than 1 metre (3 feet) high, and a double culvert passing under the road at the end of the field is further evidence that a significant stream sometimes passes here. When water does flow, it is clear and pure – difficult to associate with the murky waters that pass through London, at the other end of the Thames Path.

Onward to Ewen

Go over a wooden footbridge near the end of the field, then over a stile and across the road, noticing to your right the houses on the outskirts of Kemble. Go through a gate and continue along the path. The river, or riverbed, is now on your right, shielded for the most part by trees and bushes, while on your left is an open field. At the end of the field, branch right with the line of the river and follow the path round to a gate leading into another field. Keep to the right, walking beside the meandering stream. In spots where it is visible, its youthful character is evident – it sparkles and gurgles, creating dancing patterns of light on its surface.

When you reach the road, cross over and turn left. Just beyond the low wall by the bridge, branch right along a path that continues by the river under dense, shady trees – so dense, in fact, that few weeds grow on the riverbed here for lack of light. The path soon emerges from the secretive glade to follow the road into Ewen. This is also where you bid the river farewell. If you are unlucky enough to have walked beside nothing but a dry riverbed so far, rest assured that the Thames awaits you in its many moods on all subsequent walks.

Walk past a farmhouse on the right and on into the village of Ewen, crossing to the left when you see a pavement. 'Ewen' comes from a Saxon word meaning 'source of a river', and has a sleepy atmosphere typical of this area. The Thames Path follows a road to the right, but this walk continues straight on to the next junction, and then turns left along the road to Coates and Siddington. If you fancy a break, go straight ahead at this junction, bearing left along the main road until you reach the Wild Duck Inn, a typical English country tavern.

Down Country Lanes

Just 100 metres (110 yards) after the turning to Coates and Siddington, the road branches. Take the left fork, and walk up a slight rise along a country lane between open fields. On the left, there is a good view across to the church and houses of Kemble. The route now follows sealed roads for about 3 kilometres (2 miles), longer than any other road walk in this book, but there is little traffic, the verges are speckled with wild flowers, and the views across fields are expansive. When you go under a disused railway arch, look out to the left as you climb up beyond it, and you will see the valley that you walked through earlier.

At the junction with the A429, turn right for a few steps, then cross over and go left up the lane beside Smerrill's Barns. The Thames & Severn Canal used to cross the road near here, via a notoriously leaky aqueduct that would douse anyone who walked under it. Between here and the entrance to Sapperton Tunnel, the canal needed to be constantly 're-puddled', or re-lined, when it was in operation, and increasing maintenance costs eventually led to its demise in 1927. You will get a closer look at the derelict canal later on this walk.

Walk up a long rise to Smerrill's Dairy on the left. Note that the house beside it is named after Lyd Well, which lies just down the hill beyond the dairy barns. Go on to the junction with the A433. Cross it with care, then take the minor road leading to Coates, bordered by low dry-stone walls. Walk on down here, passing a large field and then a dense wood on the left. About 100 metres (110 yards) past a gate house (dated 1877), and just beyond a wooden gateway, go left through a gap in a dry-stone wall at the beginning of a field. Walk down to the left of the field, where there may be sheep grazing, and cross a stile. As you cross the second field, you get glimpses of Trewsbury House to the left through the dense woods surrounding it. The house stands on the site of an old fort. At the end of the field, pass some abandoned stables on the right, go through a barred metal gate and turn left for a few steps until you reach a signpost. The route back to the source of the Thames lies straight ahead, but you might like to turn right to look at the dried-up bed of the Thames & Severn Canal, or even make a diversion to the intriguing Sapperton Tunnel.

Option – Sapperton Tunnel

This diversion is not circular, but is well worth it if you have time to spare. Go right at the signpost to Tunnel House and walk along the banks of the derelict Thames & Severn Canal. This short walk passes the remains of Coates' round house, one of five built along the 46.5 kilometres (29 miles) of the canal for the 'lengthmen' who maintained it, and then enters an area of dense tree cover before arriving at the eastern entrance to Sapperton Tunnel. The 4 kilometre (2½ miles) tunnel was a miraculous feat of engineering when it was completed in 1789, but the canal soon lost traffic to the Wilts & Berks Canal which opened in 1810, and no barge passed through the tunnel after 1911. The barges used to be propelled through the tunnel by 'leggers', who lay on their backs and 'walked' along the roof of the tunnel. The Tunnel House Inn, beside the tunnel entrance, was originally built for construction workers, and is now a wonderfully quirky watering hole in the middle of nowhere.

Back to the Source

Back on the main route of the walk, follow the stony farm track between tall bushes down to a field. Go over a high wooden stile to the left of a gate and along the left of the field. Cross another high stile, where you should see a big barn on the hill to the right. Keep to the left and then go over a low stile, which brings you into the glade beside the official source of the river, where the walk began. Retrace your steps across the field to the right, cross the railway line and return to the car or the station; or retire to the Thames Head Inn to reflect on the beginning of England's principal river.

Ashton Keynes

Summary: This is one of the longest and most enjoyable rambles in this book, since you are surrounded by water for much of the way. Beginning at Neigh Bridge on the outskirts of Somerford Keynes, the path passes between lakes in the Cotswold Water Park on its way to Ashton Keynes. Here it branches away from the Thames, going north between more lakes, to take a look at the progress of the River Churn in South Cerney. Finally, the route heads west across fields and around more lakes, skirts the northern fringe of Somerford Keynes, then returns along the Thames.

Location:	146 kilometres (91 miles) west of London; 71 kilometres (44 miles) west of Oxford.
Visitor attractions:	Lakes of Cotswold Water Park; bridges at Ashton Keynes; River Churn at South Cerney.
Start/Finish:	Neigh Bridge, just south of Somerford Keynes. OS Explorer map 169, GR 947018.
Access:	(***by car***) Somerford Keynes lies about 6.5 kilometres (4 miles) south of Cirencester. Turn west off the A419 about 5 kilometres (3 miles) southeast of Cirencester and follow the B4696 between lakes until it turns left to Ashton Keynes. Go straight ahead on Spine Road. About 2.5 kilometres (1½ miles) later, turn right at a junction towards Neigh Bridge and Somerford Keynes, then immediately left into the car park/camping area. (***by bus***) Take a 92 bus (Andybus) from Cirencester to Somerford Keynes. Walk south out of the village, following a bend to the right, to Neigh Bridge.
Length:	13.5 kilometres (8¼ miles).
Time:	4 hours.
Refreshments:	The White Hart Inn at Ashton Keynes; the George Inn, the Eliot Arms Hotel and several restaurants in South Cerney; the Baker's Arms in Somerford Keynes.
Pathway status:	Firm gravel drives and tracks; grass and dirt tracks; pavements and sealed roads.
Best time to visit:	Since this walk is so near the source, the stream is more impressive after a period of rain.

Background

Just 8 kilometres (5 miles) from its source, the Thames is clear, generally shallow, and skips playfully across grasses and reeds on the riverbed. For much of this walk, it is dwarfed by the vast lakes of the Cotswold Water Park alongside it. The area is rich in gravel, which is being excavated for road building, and the resulting quarries are being converted into lakes, some for use as wetland sanctuaries for wildlife,

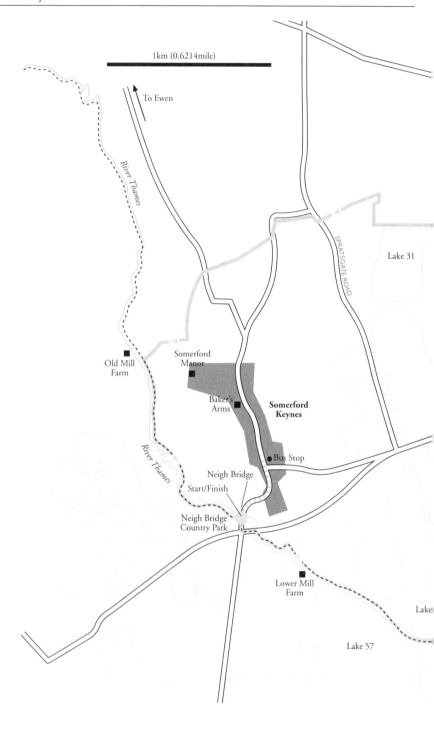

1km (0.6214mile)

To Ewen

River Thames

SPRATSGATE ROAD

Lake 31

Old Mill Farm

Somerford Manor

Baker's Arms

Somerford Keynes

River Thames

Bus Stop

Neigh Bridge

Start/Finish

Neigh Bridge Country Park

Lower Mill Farm

Lake

Lake 57

particularly birds, and some for recreation. Here you can sail, canoe, water or jet ski, fish or ride horses. Organized walks and talks are held throughout the year. Call (01825) 642 694 for further information.

The walk passes through two villages, Ashton Keynes and South Cerney, and skirts another, Somerford Keynes. Somerford Keynes is mentioned in a Saxon charter of 685, and its church (All Saints) has a Saxon doorway. All three villages have something of a timeless atmosphere, particularly Ashton Keynes, with its old stone cottages. The River Churn, whose source is claimed by some to be the true source of the Thames (see page 14), flows through South Cerney, every bit as attractive and lively as the Thames.

The Walk

Through a Water Wonderland

Turn right out of the car park or walk south from Neigh Bridge for 50 metres (55 yards), until you reach a crossroads. Turn left on to Spine Road, which goes through the heart of the Cotswold Water Park. After a few strides, you can see the infant river passing under the road and disappearing to the right, giving a tantalizing glimpse of its clear waters. Shortly beyond the bridge, turn right into a narrow country lane, which has a huge lake on its left. After about 100 metres (110 yards), the river suddenly appears on your right from beneath the boughs of an ash tree as a narrow, sparkling stream.

After passing Lower Mill Farm on the right, continue along the gravel drive. Soon, another lake appears on the right, and together with the river the surroundings become a water wonderland. At the end of the gravel drive, cross the river over a tiny bridge so that it is now on your left. The path bends round to the left, passing lake 42 on the left and lake 57 on the right (all lakes are numbered in the water park). The river's course is now due east to Ashton Keynes and the path follows beside it all the way.

When you come across another path, with a signpost pointing right to Poole Keynes, go straight ahead and over a stile. You will now follow a particularly lovely stretch of the river, still shallow but getting wider. Large trees overhang the broad gravel path and river. Keep going straight ahead with the river on your left, past a footbridge and a road bridge across it. Cross a wooden footbridge, where some of the river's water trickles away to the right. Soon you come out on to a road, where you should continue straight ahead, towards the first houses of Ashton Keynes.

The Village of 20 Bridges

Soon both the river and path become narrower to squeeze past the stone cottages of Ashton Keynes. The river disappears under a wall but then reappears, just one metre wide and bordered by a neat verge, and flows through the village. It passes under a tiny double culvert along Church Walk, at the end of which there is a market cross. Most of the river flows to the right here. If you want to make a brief diversion, follow it down the High Road. You will see some of Ashton Keynes' 20 bridges, which give access to the houses bordering the tiny river; and if you need refreshment at this point, visit the White Hart Inn, 100 metres (110 yards) down on the left.

To follow this walk, however, turn left at the end of Church Walk, walk on for a few metres, then turn right into Back Street. Carry on until you reach a sharp bend to the right, just beyond Pilgrim Cottage on the left. Here, go straight on, down a gravel drive beside a garage and along a very narrow gravel path to the right of a house. This leads between old stone cottages, where the path is flanked by thin stone slabs. After Fox Cottage, the last house of Ashton Keynes, go through a kissing gate and turn left on to an enclosed path, with tall firs on the right and a lake behind them.

Lakeside Wandering

When you emerge from the enclosed path, keep going straight ahead along the west side of lake 76. At the top corner, turn right and walk along the northern border of the lake, where you may see swans, ducks or Canada geese bobbing on its surface. When you reach a left turning, follow it through a field and over a stile into a grassy picnic area and car park. Go right, leaving the grassy area through a gap in the trees, then turn left. You soon come out on to Spine Road.

Cross the road and go over a stile into a delightful sheltered arbour. A firm gravel path takes you between lakes 25 and 26, then comes out by the lakeside. Turn right here and follow the broad gravel drive around the east and north side of the lake. On the west bank, you will notice sailing boats and a marina, behind which are the gravel processing works. Continue down the broad drive until it finishes and becomes a narrow path crossing a wide, grassy area. Follow this as it branches away from the lake and goes down an avenue between tall hedges. There are gravel works on either side here, so unfortunately you may hear heavy machinery.

Checking out the Churn

The path comes to a junction with a bridleway, beside a barrier. Turn right here, cross a footbridge over a stream, and continue to the end, passing the first houses of South Cerney on the left. At the end of the bridleway, cross Broadway Lane and turn left towards the centre of South Cerney. Continue down the street, then turn right at the war memorial. Take the next left, a road signposted to Preston and Cirencester. You soon reach a cluster of shops and refreshment options by the bridge over the River Churn, including the Eliot Arms Hotel, a 16th-century Cotswold stone house with a riverside patio.

As with the Thames, the flow of the Churn depends on how much rain has fallen in recent weeks, but it frequently rushes and gurgles under the bridge with great energy here. Since the River Churn has its source both further from the sea and higher above sea level than the Thames, there remains the nagging doubt that early cartographers got it wrong, and that this tributary is in fact the real Thames. The tussle between the two sources ends at Cricklade (walk 3), where the two rivers meet.

Cross the bridge and turn left. Follow the road between houses and back across the river over a miniature humpback bridge. The small scale of the river gives the feeling of walking through a toytown, much as the Thames does in Ashton Keynes. Turn right on to a footpath immediately after the first house on the right. After just 50 metres (55 yards), where the path bends round to the left between houses, take a grassy track to the right. This goes alongside the river and is usually choked with weeds. Pass a few houses on the left, then turn left away from the Churn along the side of a field.

Wetlands in the Making

When you reach a road, go straight ahead, past several cottages on the left (one of which is called Dirty Pig Cottage). Just before a lane marked Langet on the left, go right over a stile and along the left side of a field. Leave this field by a stone stile about 20 metres (22 yards) from the left corner, beside a telegraph pole. Walk on with farmhouses to your right until you reach a double stile. Shortly afterwards, go over another stile beside a gate, which leads out to a road.

Cross the road, go over a stile and straight ahead through a bumpy field. After another stile, the path goes slightly left to reach the left corner of the next field. Go through a gate and over a stream, then turn right to walk along the north side of a recently made lake, popular with birds. At the end of this lake, go over a footbridge, then turn left beside an enormous gravel pit, destined to become another large lake soon. The path takes you along the east and south sides of the pit, but where it turns northward up the west side, go through a gap in the hedge on the left, then turn right to stroll round the north side of lake 31. There is a pleasant panorama over this lake, particularly in the evening, and a bench in the middle of the north bank provides a good viewing point.

At the northwest corner of the lake, leave the lakeside path and cross a stile on your right. Keep going right along a broad grassy avenue, bordered by a high bank. When the avenue comes to an end and the bank bends to the right, look for a gap in the hedge on the left and cross a stile into a wood, where you may spot rabbits in the dense undergrowth. Follow the path to the left, which then leads you out of the wood, over a stile and along the right-hand side of a field. Go over a wooden footbridge and along the right-hand side of the next field too, then over a stile to a road.

Cross the road and go over a stile straight ahead. Look for a gap between holly bushes on your right, and go down an enchanting path sheltered by giant limes and chestnuts. This brings you out near the end of a field. A few steps to the right, there is a stile next to a barred gate. This leads you on to a road, where you turn left. Cross over, then after 50 metres (55 yards) go over a stile beside a signpost pointing to Somerford Keynes. If you would like to explore the village rather than return via the Thames, you could carry straight along the road here, which takes you there directly.

Back to the Infant Thames

Walk along the right of a field up a slope. You can see the rooftops of Somerford Keynes to your left. At the top, cross the road, veering slightly to the right, and enter another field. Take the farm track that slopes diagonally left down towards the buildings of Somerford Manor. Just before you reach the gates in front of the buildings, turn right following a signpost to Ewen. Leave the field by a stile beside a barred gate. Make for the house ahead of you, then go to the left of it beside a hedge and over a footbridge. The building to the right is Old Mill Farm, which borders the Thames, just 20 metres (22 yards) in front of you.

Walk up to the river, which may be little more than a trickle, and turn left. Cross a stile and continue. The river should be on your right, although it is frequently blocked from view by trees and bushes. Ignore the first footbridge that you see and continue to the end of this field, then along the right of the next. When you come to another footbridge, go over it, and you will see a lake directly ahead. This is Neigh Bridge Country Park, and the last lake to be seen on this walk. From here, you simply need to turn left and follow the Thames as it twists and turns its way down to Neigh Bridge.

Cricklade

Summary: This walk begins in the first town beside the Thames – Cricklade. It goes down the High Street and passes the enormous church of St Sampson's before heading east to follow the infant stream. It then crosses the river and goes north through fields to the village of Latton, before returning along the disused North Wilts Canal to the Thames. The final stretch back into Cricklade passes the ancient North Meadow, where the rare snake's head fritillary can be seen in spring.

Location:	139 kilometres (87 miles) west of London; 50 kilometres (31 miles) west of Oxford.
Visitor attractions:	Over 1,000 years of history at Cricklade; riverside trails; village of Latton; disused North Wilts Canal; snake's head fritillary in North Meadow.
Start/Finish:	Town Hall on Cricklade High Street. OS Explorer map 169, GR 099934.
Access:	(*by car*) Cricklade lies just west of the A419 between Swindon and Cirencester. Park in the Town Hall car park at the south end of the High Street, just north of the junction of the B4040 and B4553.
	(*by train/bus*) Take a train from Paddington to Swindon, then a 51 bus (Stagecoach Cirencester) to Cricklade.
Length:	9 kilometres (5½ miles).
Time:	3 hours.
Refreshments:	Several pubs, cafés and restaurants in Cricklade High Street.
Pathway status:	Pavements; dirt tracks; farm tracks; country paths. Can get overgrown.
Best time to visit:	Late April or May, when the snake's head fritillary is in flower in North Meadow.

Background

Cricklade, the first town along the Thames, is situated at the river's confluence with the Churn. It was founded when the Romans built the Ermin Way between Silchester and Gloucester, which crossed the river here. In Saxon days, Alfred the Great made it into a fortified town with earth ramparts. Later, stone walls were added, but these were destroyed by King Canute in 1016. From 979 to 1100 the town had its own mint, but it never developed into a large community. Today it remains a quiet town with the motto 'in loco delicioso', meaning 'in a delightful place'. Not everyone agrees, however. In 1821 the journalist William Cobbett called it 'that villainous hole' (a reference to corrupt politicians), and James Thorn, another 19th-century chronicler, said it was 'dull to look at, to live in and to talk about'. Modern visitors are likely to find its rural atmosphere relaxing and refreshing.

There was once a wharf at Cricklade, visited by the small barges that made the journey this far, but it fell into disuse when the Thames & Severn and North Wilts canals were built in the late 18th and early 19th centuries. Use of the canals was short lived, due to the arrival of the railways, and these days the river around Cricklade is a haven for plant life and birds.

The Walk

Historic Cricklade
Turn right from the Town Hall and walk up the High Street towards the river. When you reach Church Lane on the left, cross over and walk down it to look at Cricklade's most distinctive building – St Sampson's Church. As you enter the churchyard, you will see the old town cross on the right. The church dates back to Saxon times, but was expanded over the years, particularly in the 16th century when the enormous, pinnacled tower was added. This is a reminder of the prosperity generated by the Cotswold wool mills. As at Lechlade (see page 33), the church is a dominant feature of the skyline for miles around, and you can use its location to judge your progress for much of this walk.

Go back to the High Street, turn left and pass the typical village shops and pubs. In front of the Vale Hotel is the Jubilee Clock, erected in 1898 to commemorate 60 years of rule by Queen Victoria. Opposite is Calcutt Street, which leads to the local museum (see Opening Times), a former Baptist chapel. It houses an eclectic mix of objects from Cricklade's past, including Roman coins, a pistol and musket, paintings of former MPs and some intriguing old photos. One shows a man standing under the town bridge in the dried-up bed of the Thames, demonstrating the river's unpredictable character.

Beside the Infant Thames
On the left at the top of the High Street is St Mary's Church, which is just as old as St Sampson's but less imposing. It also has a 14th-century cross standing beside it. Turn right into Abingdon Court Lane just before the church, and where the lane bends right into Thames Lane, go left. At the end of the road are three tracks. To the left of the right-hand track, there is a stile over a large stone slab beside a brick wall. Cross it and go left across a short field, then over another stile. The Thames now appears to your left, bordered by willows. Walk along the bumpy, rutted track beside the river.

At the end of the field, cross a concrete bridge over a stream, and go left to follow the river. From here there is a fine view back upstream, with willows hanging low over the water and the distinctive spire of St Sampson's on the left. Cross a wooden stile, pass under the large road bridge that carries the A419 along the route of the Ermin Way, and cross another stile beyond the bridge. You are now heading for open country and are free to enjoy one of the river's lonelier stretches, which is dense with reeds and plant life. Go through gates and over a small footbridge, then pass a curious concrete arched bridge carrying pipes across the river. Cross another couple of stiles and then go left over a wooden footbridge to the north bank, pausing to take in the attractive views both up- and downstream.

A Difficult Path at Eysey

After crossing the river, you can see a solitary building almost directly ahead. This is Eysey Manor. Do not go towards it, but go diagonally left to leave the field over a stile beside a stream. Go up the left side of the next field and over another stile into a dense thicket of willows, ash, nettles and brambles. The next 100 metres (110 yards) may be something of an assault course, and if you carry a machete in your pack, now may be the time to use it. The rarely used path follows the stream as closely as possible to another stile, then continues directly northwards to a cottage on the opposite bank.

Cross a sealed road and go past the cottage, then turn left over a footbridge. Turn right, then shortly afterwards cross a stile into a large field. Keep to the right of the field, beside a hawthorn hedge that shields a view of the stream. Go over a wooden fence beside a barred gate into another field and continue up its right-hand side until you reach another barred gate and fence. Climb over this fence on to a sealed road beside Sheeppen Bridge. Cross the road and go straight ahead through the undergrowth, then over a stile into a field.

To the Village of Latton

Keep to the left of the following three fields, moving away from the stream on the right. There is no discernible track but stiles between the fields should reassure you that you are on a public footpath. Leave the third field through a wooden gate, cross a rutted track and go over a stile. The farm buildings and houses of Latton are now visible on the left. Go diagonally left across the field to a stile about halfway down, directly in front of the farm buildings. Turn right after the stile and follow the fence to a stile beside a barred gate. Cross it, turn left, pass through a gate and walk along a sealed road into Latton.

Latton is a small, ancient village on the route of the Ermin Way. It has an attractive Norman church dedicated to St John the Baptist, with tumble-down tombs tottering at odd angles in the graveyard. Walk straight down the main road of the village, where you might not see a soul. At the end, there is a medieval preaching cross on an island in the middle of the road. Turn right and walk about 50 metres (55 yards), then cross over and go down a broad sealed drive to the left of a house. Follow this up and over the A419, via a modern bridge with a high guard fence.

Along a Disused Canal

Once over the A419, leave the road as it bends round to the left, instead carrying straight on and over a concrete bridge. The weed-choked stream flowing under it is in fact the Churn, shortly to merge with the Thames at Cricklade. After the bridge, follow the farm track to the right, then take the left of two tracks. This appears to be a private drive leading to a house. However, just to the left of the entrance, a footpath leads round the side of the house to follow along the banks of the disused North Wilts Canal.

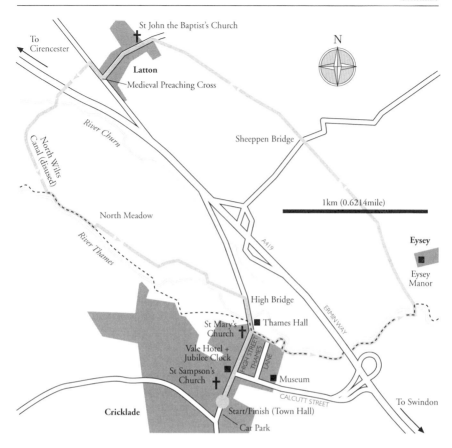

Dense bushes, mostly hawthorn, have grown around the old canal, closing in on the path. You may well see rabbits darting through the thriving vegetation. The canal is now dry, but after its opening in 1819 it offered a convenient route from the Thames & Severn Canal to the Wilts & Berks Canal near Swindon. Barges laden with coal would pass this way en route to London, avoiding the treacherous reaches of the Upper Thames. However, the huge investment and manpower involved in its construction were wasted, as railways, built in the mid-19th century, soon offered a cheaper and faster method of transportation.

The canal bends to the left through an attractive arbour of trees and bushes. Shortly, however, you need to go over a stile by a broken and moss-covered brick wall, then over a wooden footbridge into a more open area. Follow the path beside the canal bed for about another 100 metres (110 yards), until you reach a gateway leading to a bridge. This bridge once carried the canal over the river, and the tiny stream passing beneath it is no less than the Thames. You now walk close to the river for most of your route back into Cricklade.

Through an Ancient Flood Meadow

Do not cross the bridge, but instead cross a stile to its left and go down into a huge meadow. This is the famous North Meadow, one of the few flood plains adjacent to the Thames that has remained undisturbed. It is used for winter grazing, and you may pass groups of horses or cows munching its rich pasture. Walk along the edge of the meadow, with the river on your right. On your left are more than 40 hectares (100 acres) of open grassland. The meadow is thick with wild flowers such as marsh marigolds, water crowfoot and celandines, but most famous is the snake's head fritillary, which blooms in late April and May. At this time of year, the purple, bell-shaped heads of this rare flower speckle the meadow with colour.

Stroll along the meadow until you reach a stile. Do not cross it, but turn left away from the river, and follow the line of the hawthorn hedge on your right. Follow the hedge round to the right with the meadow on your left, and ignore the first wooden footbridge on your right. Towards the end of the meadow, the track bears right and takes you over a wooden footbridge and into a clump of bushes. Cross a stile, then go over the last open corner of the meadow and head to the right of an old stone bridge. This is called High Bridge, though in fact it is so low that the road hardly rises at all. Turn right away from the bridge and the meadow, and walk back into Cricklade. On your right, you will pass the site of a former priory, long since converted into houses, on your left is Thames Hall. As you enter Cricklade High Street, look out for the Thames passing under you, so small and insignificant it would be easy to miss. Continue along the High Street to the Town Hall on the left at the end.

Plate 1: *The official source of the Thames, as decided by the Conservators of the River Thames in 1958, is marked by a stone tablet and ash tree. It is usually dry (see page 15).*

Plate 2: Small island in the River Churn at South Cerney. Some people believe that the Churn is in fact the real River Thames (see page 25).

Plate 3: With features that date from Anglo-Saxon times, St John the Baptist's Church at Latton appears as if time has left it behind (see page 30).

Plate 4: Old Father Thames, which originally stood at the river's source, now keeps a watchful eye over the waters at St John's Lock in Lechlade (see page 34).

Plate 5: The River Leach passes under a house before joining the Thames (see page 34).

Plate 6: Narrow boat passing under a footbridge near the village of Kelmscot (see page 37).

Plate 7: Despite its name, Newbridge, built in the 13th century, was once considered the oldest bridge on the Thames. Radcot Bridge now makes this claim (see page 42).

Lechlade

Summary: For anyone who wants to become truly acquainted with the Thames, a visit to Lechlade, the navigable limit of the river, is unmissable. This short walk passes through the centre of the small market town with its coaching inns and antique shops. It then heads across fields to the confluence of the Thames and Coln rivers, where the Thames & Severn Canal once joined the flow. After a brief diversion to look at an isolated 11th-century church, the route follows the Thames under Ha'penny Bridge and along to St John's Lock. This is the first lock on the river, and a statue of Old Father Thames reclines here. Finally, the path passes the site of a former priory and returns to the centre of Lechlade via a delightful arbour and Shelley's Walk. Though the walk is short, it enables you to set foot in three counties (Gloucestershire, Wiltshire and Oxfordshire).

Location:	144 kilometres (90 miles) west of London; 37 kilometres (23 miles) west of Oxford.
Visitor attractions:	Antique shops; confluence of Thames and Coln Rivers; St John the Baptist Church at Inglesham; Ha'penny Bridge; first lock on river; statue of Old Father Thames; Shelley Walk; St Lawrence's Church; Buscot Park (option).
Start/Finish:	In the Market Place beside St Lawrence's Church in the centre of Lechlade. OS Explorer map 170, GR 996214.
Access:	(*by car*) Park in the car park by the New Memorial Hall, a short distance north of Lechlade town centre on the A361. Turn right out of the car park and walk down to the Market Place. There is also a short-stay (two hour) car park at the Market Place itself. (*by train/bus*) Take a train from Paddington to Swindon, then a 77 bus (Stagecoach Swindon), which stops in the Market Place in Lechlade.
Length:	5.5 kilometres (3½ miles).
Time:	1½ hours.
Refreshments:	The Trout Inn by St John's Lock; several pubs, restaurants and tea houses in Lechlade.
Pathway status:	Pavements; country paths; towpath.

Background

The small market town of Lechlade, which snuggles around the towering spire of St Lawrence's Church, is the epitome of a rural English community. Its name comes from the River Leach, which joins the Thames just downstream of St John's Lock. The town existed before written records were kept, and even in the 16th century was described by John Leland, librarian to Henry VIII, as 'a praty old toune'. Lechlade is situated on a rare patch of firm ground; there are very few beside the river upstream of Oxford, the reason why there is little riverside habitation for the next 48 kilometres (30 miles) downstream. Up until the mid-19th century, the town had an important commercial wharf, and barges weighed down with stone, tin, iron, coal, cheese and cider began their journey to London from here. Since then it has attracted pleasure boaters during the summer months. There are some fine coaching inns in the town centre, and several antique shops, including an 'Antiques Arcade' that is a veritable maze of stalls.

St John's Lock is home to the statue of Father Thames, and is the first of 45 locks between the source and London. These locks, which allow boats to pass safely over changes in water level, give the river much of its sedate, unhurried character. Their presence has also necessitated lock keepers, the true guardians of the Thames for generations.

The Walk

Stepping Over Stiles

From the Market Place, walk west past the New Inn and Red Lion, to a traffic light by the junction with Thames Street. Resist the temptation to turn left down to the river, and continue on Fairford Road, past the Antiques Arcade and an unusual shop that sells Christmas items year-round. Soon you are beyond the shops of Lechlade and passing modern houses. The road bends to the right, and there is a lay-by on the left. Just beyond the lay-by, look out for a knee-high stone at the end of a tall fir hedge. Step over it into a narrow passage that is almost concealed by low-hanging tree branches.

The path passes between gardens, over a stile by a narrow brook, then across several small fields separated by shallow streams. Each one is crossed by a wooden footbridge with a stile at each end. Don't let the sound of all these stiles worry you, as most of them are only ankle-high. As you enter a larger field, the track runs to the right by a hedge. You may catch a glimpse of the tops of boats or fishermen's rods on your left, as the path is now running parallel to the river. At the end of this field, cross another stile, which brings you out on to a sealed road at a bend. Go straight ahead for about 10 metres (11 yards), then turn left over yet another stile beside a barred metal gate marked 'Round House and Cottage'.

Follow a wide gravel farm track with a tall hedge to your left and an open field to your right, and cross a cattle grid. When you reach a barred gate marked 'private', go left along a footpath which bends round sharply. On your right there is a wide stream, which is in fact the River Coln, just before it joins the Thames. There are often swans and ducks paddling where the rivers join, and the delicate willows drooping low over the water make a harmonious composition. The path leads you over a wooden footbridge to the south bank of the Thames. Pause on the bridge and look upstream to enjoy the view of the cottage and creeper-covered round house behind it. This marks the point where the Thames & Severn Canal (see page 18) used to join the Thames, until its closure in 1927. There is also a good view downstream towards Lechlade, with its impressive church tower.

Stepping Back in Time

At your discretion, you can now make a short detour away from the circular route, to visit a very special church that time seems to have left behind. Turn right and walk upstream along the Thames, crossing a small footbridge where the river swings around in a wide bend. From here, follow a path that heads across the field to the left of the church. A house lies ahead. Skirt around the left of its large garden, then over a stile to a sealed road. Turn right, and you will soon find the Church of St John the Baptist on your right.

From the outside, there is nothing very unusual about the building; but as soon as you step inside, you will see that the flagstones of the floor have been worn down over many centuries. The earliest parts of the church date back to Saxon times, and much of the nave and chancel date from the 13th century. However, what really gives the church its ancient feel are the remnants of wall paintings that date from the 13th to 19th centuries; the wooden screens and unusual box pews, which are about 400 years old; and a striking carving of the Virgin and Child, around 1,000 years old. The church was restored in the late 19th century with the help of William Morris (see page 42), who lived a short distance away at Kelmscot and had a great appreciation for the art and architecture of the Middle Ages.

Under Ha'penny Bridge

Retrace your steps from the church to the Round House, then continue walking downstream along the right bank of the river. Shortly after the wooden footbridge that you crossed earlier, you will probably pass the first boats moored on the Thames, for this is the head of the river for all water transport apart from canoes. You may also pass anglers here, and almost certainly swans and ducks. The path goes over a small concrete bridge into Riverside Park. The opposite bank is lined with tall poplars, behind which is a marina full of boats.

Soon the path passes under Ha'penny Bridge, built in 1792, which spans the river with an attractive arch. It may be busy here, as you are only a few steps from Lechlade town centre. As you come out on the other side of the bridge, look back to see the small toll house attached to its downstream side. This was where the half penny toll was once collected.

As you walk away from the bridge, following the river's lazy bends, the views open out and the surroundings rapidly become peaceful. The grassy banks are imprinted with dark circles that look remarkably like fairy rings, so take care as you tread. This tranquil stretch of the river is favoured by swans and ducks. You may even see herons, which stand statue-like in the shallows, or glide off with a graceful flap of their enormous wings.

The Thames as Highway and Barrier

Looking back at the town from downstream, the view is of a timeless English landscape. In *The Historic Thames* (c. 1900), British writer and politician Hilaire Belloc noted that '…there are dozens of reaches on the upper Thames where little is in sight save the willows, the meadows, and a village church tower, which present exactly the same aspect today as they did when that church was first built.' This sense of timelessness is one of the great joys of walking the Thames above Oxford.

In Belloc's book, he states that there are two principal ways in which a river gains historic importance: as a highway, and as a line of defence. At Lechlade, there is ample evidence of the Thames' use as a continuous highway from here to the sea. As you walk on towards St John's Lock, you will also see a bizarre example of how it was viewed as a line of defence as late as the Second World War. On the north bank, there is a hexagonal concrete block with narrow slits at head height. This is a pill box, built in 1940 in preparation for a possible land invasion by the German army. Fortunately, the invasion never materialized, but this pill box, and many others like it between here and Oxford, is a reminder of a dark phase in England's turbulent history. The Thames still acts as a boundary for administrative purposes. At this point, the north bank of the river is in Gloucestershire and the south bank is in Wiltshire. Then, shortly before St John's Lock, you step into Oxfordshire.

Meeting Father Thames

Walk through the gate into the grounds of St John's Lock. This is one of the most significant spots on the whole river, not only because it is the first of many locks between here and Teddington, but also because it is home to a flamboyant statue of Old Father Thames. Originally sculpted for the Great Exhibition of 1851, the long-haired figure with a flowing beard reclines beside barrels, which represent the cargo once carried on the river. He also holds a spade, which represents the digging of locks to make the river navigable. The statue was moved here from Thames Head in 1974 to protect it from vandals.

Before you leave the lock, look for some model houses on the island opposite the statue. Then climb the steps and go through a gateway on to the road. Cross with care, turn left and go over St John's Bridge. On the other side is the Trout Inn. This stands on the site of St John's Priory, established in 1246 and dissolved in 1475, which gave its name to the bridge, the lock, and the tiny church that you may have visited at Inglesham. The inn, with its low, timbered ceiling, is cosy and welcoming.

If you would like to take a look at the River Leach, turn right down the Kelmscot Road just beyond the Trout Inn. Walk about 100 metres (110 yards) to a small bridge, where to the left you can see the river flowing under a house and through a garden. Otherwise, cross the road from the Trout and look for the entrance to a narrow path, just before a board welcoming you back to Gloucestershire, which may be concealed by vegetation. Cross a narrow stream, and you will be greeted by the sight of a long arbour, created by willows and hawthorns. The firm path is raised above the level of the fields on either side, an indication that these meadows are prone to flooding.

A Stroll Down Shelley's Walk

The beautiful bower that lies ahead is part of an ancient walkway linking the priory with St Lawrence's Church. When the path leaves the shelter of the trees, cross a stile and continue across an open meadow towards the church spire. You can catch a last look at the river on your left, then pass a school, go through a metal kissing gate, and cross Wharf Lane into the churchyard. The path here is known as Shelley's Walk. It is named after a poem penned in 1815, which sings the praises of the lofty spire. A plaque commemorating this is set into the wall on the right, near the end of the passage. This church, which has been in sight for most of the walk, is even more impressive close up, with its imposing tower and crumbling gargoyles. Inside, its large windows make it bright and spacious. It has hardly been altered since it was built in the 1470s, and exudes an aura of great age – a fitting end to this historic walk.

Option – Buscot Park

Buscot Park lies just 4.5 kilometres (3 miles) from Lechlade on the A417 towards Faringdon. There is a strong Italian influence in the design of both house and gardens, which were built in the 1770s. In the late 19th century, the park was bought by Alexander Henderson, the first Lord Faringdon and a great patron of the arts. As a result, the house has a stunning collection of paintings by Rembrandt, Reynolds, Gainsborough, Sutherland and the pre-Raphaelites Rossetti and Burne-Jones. The *Legend of the Briar Rose*, by Burne-Jones, occupies four large panels and is of breathtaking beauty. The Water Garden and Four Seasons Walled Garden add plenty of interest outside.

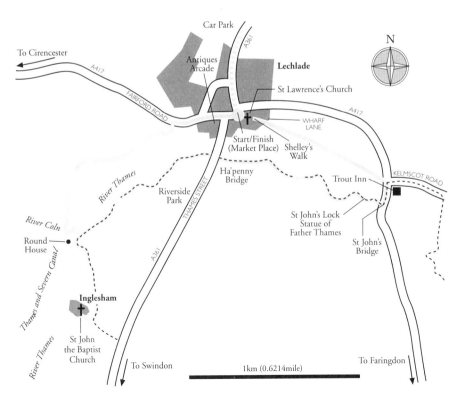

Radcot and Kelmscot

Summary: This is a walk for when you really want to get away from it all. From Radcot Bridge, it follows a rarely used path across fields to Eaton Hastings, where the church has some beautiful pre-Raphaelite stained glass windows. From there it climbs slightly, then dips down to cross the river at Eaton Footbridge. The return to Radcot follows the meandering river all the way, passing Kelmscott Manor, the home of William Morris (1834–96), and quiet reaches near Grafton Lock.

Location:	120 kilometres (75 miles) west of London; 35 kilometres (22 miles) west of Oxford.
Visitor attractions:	Radcot Bridge; Church of St Michael and All Angels, Eaton Hastings; Kelmscott Manor (option); quiet stretches of infant Thames.
Start/Finish:	Island on Thames beside Radcot Bridge. OS Explorer map 170, GR 285996.
Access:	(*by car*) Radcot Bridge crosses the Thames on the A4095 between Faringdon and Witney, west of Oxford. Drive over the first of two parts to the bridge, then turn into the car park on the island opposite the Swan Hotel.
	(*by bus*) Unfortunately, Radcot Bridge is not served by any public transport. Take a number 18 bus (Steve's Travel) from Oxford to Clanfield, which lies just over 1.5 kilometres (1 mile) north of Radcot on the A4095, then walk south to the bridge.
Length:	10.5 kilometres (6½ miles).
Time:	4 hours.
Refreshments:	The Swan Hotel, beside Radcot Bridge; the Plough Inn at Kelmscot.
Pathway status:	Country paths (sometimes indistinct); dirt tracks.
Route notes:	Parts of the outward route may get overgrown, and farmers sometimes plough across the line of footpaths, making for a muddy trek. Several of the basic stiles linking fields lack cross-bars, so might pose problems for less agile walkers.
Best time to visit:	If you would like to look around Kelmscott Manor, which is highly recommended, it is only open on Wednesdays or occasional Saturdays in Summer (see Opening Times).

Background

There are two bridges at Radcot. One is smaller, single-spanned, and carries river traffic (with difficulty – note how its arch is scarred). It was built in 1787 along with the cut creating the island. The larger one, with three arches, is now acknowledged to be the oldest on the Thames. Its piers are thought to be 12th-century; the two outer, pointed arches are probably 14th century. The central, rounded arch was repaired much later. The warm honey-coloured stone comes from the Taynton Quarry, north of Radcot. There was once a large wharf on the north bank of the river, where this same stone was loaded on to barges and shipped to Oxford and London. The Strong family, who owned the quarry in the 17th century, were close friends of the architect Sir Christopher Wren; as a result, the stone was used to build St Paul's Cathedral in London as well as some of Oxford's colleges.

The bridge was the scene of a battle in the 14th century, when the Earl of Oxford was trapped by the forces of Henry Bolingbroke, and he only escaped by plunging into the Thames. There was also a Civil War skirmish here in 1645, when Royalists managed to repel a Parliamentarian attack.

The Walk

A Wilderness Trek

Before setting out on a trek into the wilderness, take a good look at the three spans of Radcot Bridge, the oldest bridge on the river. Notice the strengthening ribs inside the arches, and the protruding 'V' shapes on the piers. On the upstream side, these are to deflect the force of the current, but from the car park you see the downstream side, where they must have been added for purely aesthetic reasons. Beside the Swan Hotel is a newer, single-span bridge. This must have been cursed many a time by both boatmen and drivers, since it is built at an awkward angle to the current and the line of the road. It is scoured and scraped both above and below.

Leave the car park, cross the road with care and turn left over the old bridge. Immediately beyond the bridge, turn right and go over a low, wooden stile into a field. Here, willows line the riverbank, cutting off any further views of Radcot Bridge. The path may be unclear, as it is little used. For a while, it follows a raised ridge behind the willows, parallel to the river. It then branches away from the river, and heads just left of an enormous pylon. Go over a stile beside a barred metal gate, and walk along the right-hand side of a field towards a farm.

In the corner of this field to the right, almost concealed beneath the boughs of a willow tree, there is a stile that leads through dense vegetation and round a pond bordered by massive, moss-covered willow trunks. When you emerge, you will see a small rusting windmill in the corner of a field. Walk through the next three fields crossing metal stiles and keeping to the right. There are farm buildings on your left, up a slight slope.

The path goes over a double wooden stile and a lichen-covered footbridge. Here, notice the rotting carcass of an ancient ash, miraculously sprouting new branches. Continue along the lower end of the next field, where you might disturb sheep or pheasants. Keep to the left of a clump of willows surrounding a shallow pond, then pass a concrete slab and a few wooden stakes in the ground. Cross another stile and go straight ahead, aiming to the right of farm buildings in the field beyond. Then go over another double wooden stile and footbridge.

From here, head to the left of the farm buildings, and leave the field over a stile.

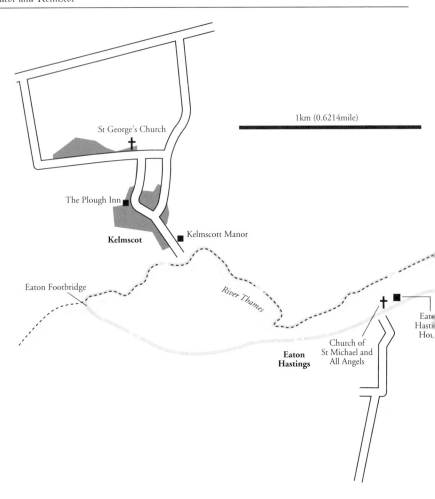

Pass a fir hedge on the right and a brick bridge over a stream. Go over a wooden stile and straight across the next field, following a line of telegraph poles. When you reach a large house surrounded by tall fir trees, pass it and head up to the right-hand corner of the field. You will emerge on to a sealed road, with the entrance to Eaton Hastings House on the right and the small Church of St Michael and All Angels in front of you, which is well worth a visit.

A Pre-Raphaelite Vision

As you enter the churchyard, note the yew trees growing there. Yews are often found in churchyards throughout the country, and are associated with immortality, perhaps because they live a long time. The church itself has some very special stained glass windows. As you enter, these are in the large window to the left (west) and the narrow lancet windows in the opposite (north) wall. They are the work of

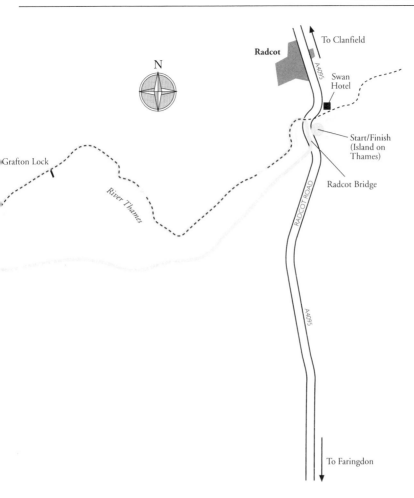

the pre-Raphaelites Edward Burne-Jones, Ford Madox Brown and William Morris, whose home at Kelmscot is just across the river. They include images of St Raphael, St Michael, St Gabriel, St Matthew and St Mary, and the colours of each glow with a wonderful richness. They are here because the owners of nearby Buscot House, Robert Campbell and Sir Alexander Henderson, were patrons of Burne-Jones's work.

Leaving the church, turn right along a sealed road for a few steps. Where the road bends left, go straight ahead, over a stile and across the middle of the next field. On the other side, cross a double stile and footbridge, then skirt some houses on the right and head across the next field, still veering slightly to the right. You may catch glimpses of the river here, which is beyond the trees to your right. Cross another stile and make for the cottage in the right-hand corner of the sloping field. Leave the field by a stile to the left of the cottage, and then veer right, going

41

down the slope towards another stile. Looking across the river, you can see the rooftops of Kelmscot village.

Cross this stile and continue down the slope towards a small cottage on the riverbank, with a line of willows on your right. There are just two more stiles to cross before you reach the cottage beside Eaton Footbridge, at the site of an old weir. Several boats are moored on a backwater here. If the going has been at all heavy so far, you can now relax, as you are about to join the well-trodden Thames Path. Cross the footbridge, turn right and wander beside the river, past one of the sentinels of the Thames, the pill boxes (see page 36), and the low-lying fields of Kelmscot. At the end of the second field after the footbridge, go through a gate and over a footbridge on to a broad, sandy path. To continue the walk, turn right; to visit Kelmscott Manor or the village, turn left.

Option – Kelmscott Manor

William Morris was a multitalented artist at odds with the Victorian society in which he lived. As a poet, novelist, painter, designer and printer, he aspired to recapture the liveliness and individuality of medieval crafts, and to escape the dehumanizing influence of industrialization. When he moved to Kelmscot in 1871 (for some reason, the village is spelled with one 't' and the manor with two), he wrote:

> *What better place than this, then, could we find,*
> *By this sweet stream that knows not of the sea,*
> *That guesses not the city's misery,*
> *This little stream whose hamlets scarce have names,*
> *This far off, lonely mother of the Thames.*

As you enter the grounds of Kelmscott Manor, you are likely to be as enthralled as Morris by your first glimpse of this cosy Elizabethan manor. Its grey gables, mullioned windows and dainty garden exude a quiet calm. It was built in 1570 and expanded in 1670, then restored by the Society of Antiquaries in 1968. Morris lived here intermittently until his death in 1896, with his beautiful wife Jane and the painter Dante Gabriel Rossetti. Rossetti's obsession with Jane Morris, who was the subject of his best-known paintings (such as *Proserpine*, 1874), must have disturbed Morris' idyll; yet he continued to work at a prodigious rate. When he died, the doctor said, 'The disease is simply…having done more work than most ten men.'

The house contains furnishings, tapestries and other designs by Morris, and enthusiastic volunteers are on hand to answer questions. If you are not in a hurry, a stroll around the village is worthwhile. The Plough Inn is an attractive spot to take refreshment, and St George's Church, where William Morris is buried along with his wife and daughters in a ridged tomb behind a bay bush, is a fine example of the kind of medieval architecture that Morris admired so much.

Return to Radcot

Retrace your steps to the riverside and follow the sandy lane until it ends. Go through a kissing gate and meander along beside the 'lonely mother of the Thames' (it appears that Morris disputed the gender of the river), with cow pastures on your left and farm buildings across the river on your right. You will see more pill boxes, somewhat overgrown, and concrete slipways running into the river. A thatched cottage on the opposite bank marks the village of Eaton Hastings (the church is just behind) and then there is no sign of habitation until you reach Grafton Lock with its pretty garden and weeping willows.

Beyond the lock, the riverside path continues for about 1.5 kilometres (1 mile), bending first to the right and then left, until the boats by Radcot Bridge come back into view. Pass under a line of pylons and beside hawthorns on a raised earthwork; then, when the river reaches the island at Radcot, follow it round to the left. Go through a gate and over a footbridge, then finally to a gate out on to the road. Go straight ahead to refresh yourself at the Swan Hotel, or turn right over the newer Radcot Bridge to return to the car park.

Northmoor and Newbridge

Summary: Like the Radcot walk, this ramble is ideal for anyone in need of peace and quiet, since you will probably meet no one but a lock keeper along the way. Beginning in the sleepy village of Northmoor, the route passes through fields and woods down to the riverside beside Newbridge, one of the oldest bridges over the Thames, and continues downstream beside the young and playful river. After snaking east and northeast through isolated meadows, the path and river pass through Northmoor Lock. Shortly beyond the lock, the path leaves the Thames to cross back over fields to Northmoor.

Location:	102 kilometres (64 miles) west of London; 17 kilometres (11 miles) west of Oxford.
Visitor attractions:	Church and cottages of Northmoor; Newbridge, one of the oldest bridges over the Thames; peaceful riverbanks; Northmoor Lock and Weir; Stanton Harcourt Manor and Gardens (option).
Start/Finish:	St Denys Church in Northmoor. OS Explorer map 180, GR 421029.
Access:	(*by car*) Just north of Newbridge, on the A415 between Abingdon and Witney, turn right behind the Rose Revived on to Moreton Lane. At the end of the road, turn right into Northmoor village and park on the right in front of the church.
	(*by bus*) Take bus 18 (Steve's Travel) from Oxford to Northmoor.
Length:	8 kilometres (5 miles).
Time:	2½ hours.
Refreshments:	The Red Lion in Northmoor; the Rose Revived and the Maybush on each side of Newbridge.
Pathway status:	Sealed roads; farm tracks; country paths.
Best time to visit:	Check opening times if you want to visit Stanton Harcourt Manor.

Background

Northmoor may not have any major historic associations, but is perhaps better for it, as its village life remains undisturbed. It is set well back from the river to avoid the flood plain. From here, the walk goes to Newbridge. These days, Radcot Bridge is generally acknowledged to be the oldest on the river, but this was not always the case. In *The Royal River* (1885), W. Senior wrote, 'The oldest, and in truth the oldest looking, stone bridge on the Thames is called Newbridge.' This name, belonging to such an old and venerable crossing, seems somewhat ironic. The bridge now bears the weight of enormous vehicles that its builders could not have even imagined. Here, the character of the river begins to change, as the waters of the River Windrush join it. It is still playful but growing fast, subtly changing from a big stream into a little river.

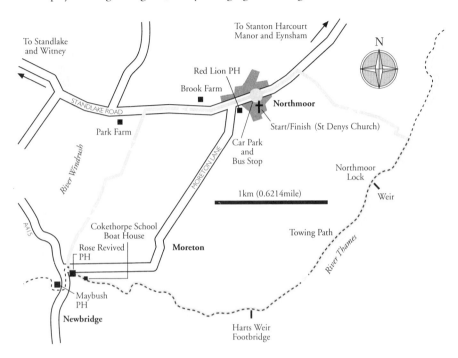

The Walk

Romance Conquers All

Before setting out towards the river, it is worth taking a look at St Denys Church, situated in the heart of Northmoor. Dating back to the 13th century, it has recently been refurbished and has a very attractive interior. The church was once the scene of a heart-warming romance that defied social conventions. In 1776, a well-to-do young student named Viscount Ashbrook went fishing on the Thames near Hart's Weir, where he met Betty Rudge, the weir-keeper's daughter. The two fell in love, but knew that an association between two people from such different classes would be frowned upon. Undeterred, the young peer had Betty trained in the social graces and the two married in St Denys Church, having overcome all objections.

On leaving the church, turn left and walk west out of the village, passing the Red Lion pub on the left and some delightful thatched cottages on the right. Pass Moreton Lane on the left, keep to the right to face oncoming traffic and continue along Standlake Road. You will pass Brook Farm on the right and other farm buildings on the left. When you reach a signpost pointing left, indicating that Newbridge is one mile away, cross over and go down a wide farm track. On your right is an open field and on your left a tall hedge.

At the end of the first field, go straight ahead, where the view across fields to the left now opens up. Follow the wide gravel path as it bends to the left through a wood of tall poplars, then sharp right along its fringe. On the left are open fields, punctuated with towering electric pylons. The path bends to the left and passes under the pylon cables.

The broad gravel path stops abruptly at the end of the field. Here, go through a gap in the willows and straight ahead through the next grassy field along a barely-discernible path. You will see a line of telegraph poles gradually converging with your course from the left. At the far side of the field, go through a narrow gap in a copse to emerge among young ash and oak trees. Cross a footbridge and a concrete ramp, then strike out diagonally left across a field, once again using the converging lines of telephone wires to guide you. Ahead is the roof of the Rose Revived pub, an indication that the path is approaching the river. Leave the field by a barred wooden gate, cross the road (Moreton Lane) and walk straight on through the pub car park.

Riverside Roaming

If you need reviving, you have the choice here of two pubs in which to rest weary legs, the Rose Revived or the Maybush. To reach the Maybush, take a slight diversion and cross Newbridge to the other bank. This ancient bridge was built around 1250 and then rebuilt in the 15th century. It proved to be of great significance during the Civil War: Oliver Cromwell captured it in 1644 and forced Charles I to retreat north from his base in Oxford. One of the best views of it is from the Thames Path just behind the Maybush, particularly in afternoon light. From here you can see the 'split-waters', V-shaped piers on the upstream side that deflect the river's flow. They are not added on the downstream side, as they are on Radcot Bridge.

From this side, you can also look for the confluence of the River Windrush with the Thames, on the north bank just above Newbridge. It is covered by dense reeds and weeds and can be barely noticeable, yet this is the largest tributary to join the Thames up to this point.

To continue the main walk, go through a gate into the garden of the Rose Revived and turn left to follow the Thames downstream. There is a fine view of Newbridge from between the willows, its pointed and ribbed arches giving it an unmistakably medieval look.

Beyond the garden of the Rose Revived is a broad lawn, then a narrow path. This leads past a boatyard and a jetty on the riverbank to open meadows beyond. When the weather is good, the stretch around to Northmoor Lock is most enjoyable as it follows the river's playful twists and turns. At the end of the first field, the path branches. The left track cuts straight across the next field, and the right hugs the meandering river. You can take either – the left track is shorter, but less interesting. The path beside the river reveals a final view back to Newbridge in the distance, then turns sharp left to follow a bend.

The river soon bends right and the path crosses a small concrete bridge over a stream. Go through a metal kissing gate, where the few houses of Moreton are visible on the left. Pass round a small, wooden shelter and go through another kissing gate into a long field. Here, you can again choose between a meandering riverside route or a direct trek across the field. A concrete pill box stands on the left, an incongruous sight in this tranquil corner of the countryside. There are often cows grazing here, which may stop and stare as you pass.

Soon the path passes a footbridge crossing the river, where Hart's Weir used to be and young Betty (see page 45) met her nobleman. The river bends to the left, taking it northeast, and continues to meander in front of some isolated properties on the opposite bank.

Back to Northmoor
The path and river soon arrive at Northmoor Lock. As you approach it, there is a fine view of an old-style 'paddle and rymer' weir to the right. This very old system regulates the flow of water manually, and only a few of the locks in these upper reaches still use it. If a boat is passing through the lock, you may notice that the lock gates are also operated manually. The first 10 locks on the Thames, up to King's Lock near Wytham, are operated in this way, while those further down are automated. These old-fashioned elements of the locks and weirs in the Upper Thames, along with the well-tended lock-keepers' cottages and gardens, only serve to increase the river's charm.

Walk on downstream, though a field. As you enter the next field, you will see an enormous pylon in front of you, and signs warning people not to fish beneath the electric cables. About 100 metres (110 yards) after these cables, just beyond a defunct stile, look for an indistinct path leading across the field to a barred gate on the left. Make for the gate and go through it. Go over a concrete bridge and along a broad gravel drive heading away from the river. Follow this drive through three fields, then go over a stile by a footpath sign. Turn left on to the road and within a couple of minutes you will be back in front of St Denys Church in Northmoor.

Option – Stanton Harcourt Manor
Situated 4 kilometres (2½ miles) north of Northmoor on the B4449, Stanton Harcourt Manor and Gardens (see Opening Times) has several interesting features. Ever since King Stephen gave the grounds to the Harcourts in the 12th century, it has remained in the same family. Little remains of the original house except the Old Kitchen and Pope's Tower. The kitchen, constructed in the late 14th century, is one of the best examples of a medieval kitchen remaining in England, with open fires in bays around the walls and smoke vents in the octagonal roof. Pope's Tower was so called because Alexander Pope (1688–1744) stayed here while translating the fifth book of Homer's *Iliad* in the summers of 1717–18. The gardens include formal lawns and flower beds, along with informal ponds and woodland.

Oxford

Summary: This walk is beside water for most of the way. It begins with an attractive stretch of the Oxford Canal, which passes the back gardens of city homes on the way to the quiet village of Wolvercote. It then meets up with the Thames at Godstow, beside the ruins of a famous nunnery. From here the walk follows the flow of the growing river beside the open pastures of Port Meadow, where Alice in Wonderland came into being, and returns to Oxford along a verdant path on Fiddler's Island.

Location:	90 kilometres (56 miles) west of London.
Visitor attractions:	Oxford Canal; Wolvercote village; Godstow Nunnery; Binsey poplars.
Start/Finish:	On the Oxford Canal by the bridge over Walton Well Road. OS Explorer map 180, GR 504073.
Access:	(*by car*) Make your way to Walton Road in Oxford, which runs parallel to the railway and Oxford Canal just northwest of the city centre. At a mini-roundabout turn west into Walton Well Road and go over a bridge on to Port Meadow. Park in the car park on the left. Walk back over the bridge and across a drive on the right, then go down a concrete ramp by a brick bridge to the canal path.
	(*by train*) From the station, turn right then right again into Cripley Road just to the west of the station. At the end of Cripley Road, bear right into Abbey Road. At the end, by a brick wall, go left down a narrow alley. Turn right over a metal bridge, then right again. Join the walk at the last section.
Length:	9 kilometres (5½ miles).
Time:	3 hours.
Refreshments:	The Red Bull and White Hart in Wolvercote; the Trout Inn at Godstow; the Perch at Binsey; many pubs, restaurants and cafés in Oxford.
Pathway status:	Towpath; pavements; country paths.

Background

On the route of this walk, you pass several places with historic and literary associations. The Oxford Canal, which stretches all the way to Hawkesbury, near Coventry, was busy with barges hauling coal and stone from the Midlands, from 1790 to 1805. The opening of the Grand Union Canal then offered a more direct route to London, and transport on the Oxford Canal declined immediately. The ruins of Godstow Nunnery, passed later in the walk, recall the legend of 'Fair Rosamund', which is steeped in jealousy and intrigue. Finally, the Thames beside

Port Meadow provided the inspiration for Lewis Carroll's world-famous story *Alice's Adventures in Wonderland*.

Despite passing within a stone's throw of Oxford's city centre, this walk is almost entirely rural, so you will need to take a separate city walk if you want a close look at the 'City of Dreaming Spires'. It is certainly a rewarding city to get to know, with its venerable colleges and energetic student population. To learn about the basics in under an hour, try the Oxford Story Exhibition on Broad Street. For a rooftop view, go up the Carfax Tower, or the tower of the Church of St Mary the Virgin on the High Street. After this, you are still left with 39 university colleges, several of the best museums, art galleries and libraries in the country, and a wide range of theatres and restaurants to visit. So allow plenty of time for your trip!

The Walk

Industry and Solitude

The first sight on this walk is somewhat uninspiring. As you come on to the towpath beside the Oxford Canal, the view opposite is of dirty brick factory buildings with smashed windows, accompanied on work days by the incessant whine of machinery. However, take heart, because from here on things improve dramatically.

Turn left to walk northwards, passing under two low brick bridges. You are soon walking among lush greenery beside the peaceful water of the canal, and glancing over into the back gardens of Oxford residents. The locals clearly appreciate their location, for many have chairs and benches conveniently positioned to overlook the canal. Brightly-coloured narrow boats may be moored here, along with small skiffs and dinghies. As you walk with the canal on your right, there is a narrow ditch on the left in which a tangle of bushes and willows thrives. Thistles, sorrel, orange balsam and willowherb blossom on the verges in summer.

Soon you reach a bridge over the canal, numbered 240. This walk follows the canal for only about 3 kilometres (2 miles), but these high numbers on its bridges give an indication of its length. The enormous efforts of engineering and manpower involved in its construction are now only appreciated by the mallards and coots that live on and around it, a few narrow boat enthusiasts. and walkers.

The towpath passes a few offices, warehouses and more residential homes, then some inhabited narrow boats with flower boxes on their roofs. Note the tiny bridges that cross the canal, which are designed so that narrow boat owners can raise and lower them easily by leverage.

Continue northward, passing under a railway bridge, along another beautiful green stretch, then under a low road bridge. You will now see two taller bridges ahead, a footbridge and a road bridge. Walk as far as the road bridge, where you will find Wolvercote Lock. This seems like a toytown version of the locks on the Thames, with its sturdy, moss-covered gates no more than a couple of metres wide. Take a few moments to look back at the view of the canal through the arch of the bridge, then climb the steps to the left and turn right along the road to Wolvercote.

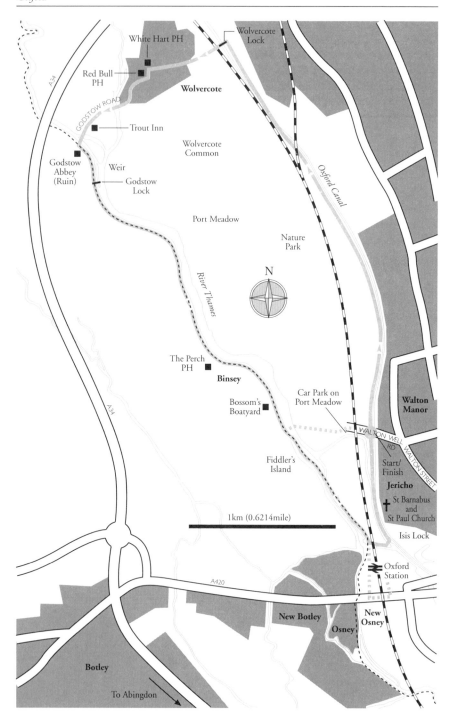

White Hart PH

Red Bull
PH

Wolvercote

Wolvercote
Lock

GODSTOW ROAD

Trout Inn

Wolvercote
Common

Godstow
Abbey
(Ruin)

Weir

Godstow
Lock

Port Meadow

Nature
Park

Oxford Canal

N

River Thames

The Perch
PH

Binsey

Bossom's
Boatyard

Car Park on
Port Meadow

**Walton
Manor**

WALTON WELL RD

WALTON STREET

Start/
Finish

Jericho

St Barnabus
and
St Paul Church

Fiddler's
Island

Isis Lock

1km (0.6214mile)

Oxford
Station

A420

New Botley

**New
Osney**

Osney

Botley

To Abingdon

Rosamund's Tale

As you emerge from the canal towpath to the pavement beside the road, there is a striking change in atmosphere. Even though the road through Wolvercote is not very busy, the noise and pollution of passing cars seems an unwelcome imposition. Walk down the slope of the bridge. From here you can see an attractive backwater behind the trees to the right, and the huge expanse of Wolvercote Common and Port Meadow to the left. Cross to the left-hand side of the road at a convenient point, and walk on through the centre of Wolvercote. Bear left at a triangular green in front of the Red Bull pub, with the White Hart on its right, then follow the Godstow Road as it snakes its way westward out of the village.

Ignore a path to the left, which leads on to Port Meadow, and go on over a bridge that crosses a beautiful backwater. If you look out to the left, a few of Oxford's spires are visible beyond Port Meadow. A few steps later, just before a bridge, you will see the overgrown roof of an old building on the left. If you are here around lunch time, there is likely to be a buzz of activity. This is the Trout Inn, once the hostel of the nearby nunnery, and now a popular pub for Oxford students. It is worth going into the garden to look at the view of Godstow Weir and the resident peacocks that strut about, and into the low-beamed interior of the pub.

Cross the bridge beside the pub. Keep an eye out for traffic, as the bridge is very narrow. Just beyond it, turn left through a gate. On the flat meadow immediately in front of you are the ruins of Godstow Nunnery. Little remains of the 12th-century building, except some perimeter walls and the shell of a chapel with windows opening out to the sky; yet its legend of Fair Rosamund gives the silent walls a romantic air. Rosamund Clifford, a woman of exceptional beauty and intellect, was being educated here when Henry II visited and fell in love with her at once. He took her as his concubine and built an underground labyrinth at Woodstock in which to hide her from his jealous queen, Eleanor of Aquitaine. According to the legend, Queen Eleanor discovered the hiding place and poisoned her rival. Rosamund died in 1176 and was buried at Godstow.

However, the story did not end there. Rosamund's tomb became an object of veneration, much to the fury of the Bishop of Lincoln. After Henry II's death, he had her bones removed from hallowed ground and interred elsewhere, so that other women might be dissuaded from following her example of unlawful love.

Walking in Wonderland

Walk on beyond the nunnery along the Thames Path and pass Godstow Lock. From here, the Thames can no longer be considered an infant river. The path continues to meander south, with open fields to the right and the expanse of Port Meadow opposite. This area of 160 hectares (400 acres) has been public land since the days of William the Conqueror in the 11th century. From 1680 to 1872 the meadow was a popular venue for horse racing, an activity that was revived on a smaller scale in the 1980s and still takes place each July. At other times, herds of horses roam over it, adding to its air of openness and freedom.

The stretch from here through Binsey and Medley to the centre of the city is home to swans, mallards and grebes, which will keep you company even if there are no other walkers about. When the weather is fine, there is certainly a magical feel to this part of the river, which in 1862 must have encouraged the Reverend Charles Dodgson (1832–98) to invent a tale for his three young charges – Lorina, Alice and Edith Liddell. It starts with a reference to rowing on the Thames:

> *All in the golden afternoon full leisurely we glide;*
> *For both our oars, with little skill, by little arms are plied,*
> *While little hands make vain pretence our wanderings to guide.*

Reverend Dodgson wrote this tale, *Alice's Adventures in Wonderland*, under the name of Lewis Carroll, and it is now one of the world's best-known children's stories. It is interesting to note in passing that, while many scholarly works have been written on the history of the Thames, the literary works influenced by the river have been written predominantly for children. Apart from *Alice's Adventures in Wonderland* and *The Wind in the Willows*, other books written near the Thames are *The Lord of the Rings* by J.R.R. Tolkien and the Narnia tales by C.S. Lewis, both of whom lived in Oxford.

Soon the path becomes shaded by giant poplar trees. These huge trees are in fact a replacement for another stand of 'Binsey poplars' that were felled in 1879. The metaphysical poet Gerard Manley Hopkins was so distraught at this that he commented, 'After comers cannot guess the beauty been'. We are fortunate that, given the chance, nature is still capable of re-establishing what has gone before.

As the name of the poplars suggests, the walk is now in the vicinity of Binsey, a small village set back from the river. The nearest building to the river is an old thatched pub called the Perch, which is signposted from the riverside path and can be approached via a short walk through dense bushes to the right. If you continue along the river for a little longer, a broad track leads off to the right, allowing a glimpse of other houses in Binsey.

Soon the path goes through Bossom's Boatyard, then over a metal footbridge on the left to a small, narrow island, where many boats are moored. If you arrived by car and want to end your walk at this stage, go over another bridge to the left and follow the clear path along the bottom corner of Port Meadow to the car park. However, it is worth continuing around the last part of the walk, which is only about another 1.5 kilometres (1 mile) long and perhaps the prettiest part of all.

Go straight ahead over a wood and concrete bridge on to Fiddler's Island, a long narrow strip of land thick with trees. The footpath is narrow but firm and bordered by lush growth. The river glides by on your right, with a line of willows on the opposite bank. A small, clear stream flows at your left, offering the perfect setting in which to complete this wander through wonderland.

Back Along the Canal

When you reach the end of the island, turn left before a metal bridge (**walkers arriving by train** join the walk here). This takes you along a sealed path and under a very low bridge beneath the railway. The water on your right is neither the Thames nor the Oxford Canal, but a cut connecting the two. The path passes a road bridge on the right leading into a new housing development on the left. Go straight ahead and over a footbridge that brings you out by the tiny Isis Lock. Like Wolvercote Lock, passed earlier on the walk, this miniature structure seems like a toy in comparison to the river locks. The Isis Lock is perhaps even more beautiful, as it is set beneath the curve of a simple bridge, number 243 of the Oxford Canal.

This walk does not cross the bridge but goes northward, straight up the canal and back to the starting point. The path is once more bordered by water on both sides, and passes several narrow boats, some of which may be awaiting repairs in the boatyard opposite. Behind the boatyard is the Italianate tower of St Barnabus and St Paul Church. A little further on are modern flats with a footbridge connecting them to this footpath. After that the ugly industrial buildings are a clear sign that you are back where you started. Go up the concrete ramp just before the next bridge, then turn left and go over the railway back to the car park.

Kennington and Radley

Summary: This pleasant stretch of the river south of Oxford has few historical associations. You are free to enjoy the natural surroundings of the riverbank as you walk from Kennington down past Sandford Lock to Radley. Here you can see Nuneham House sitting proudly on a hilltop before you pass through Radley village and the grounds of Radley College. The walk ends by passing through woodland and returning via the back lanes of Kennington.

Location:	93 kilometres (58 miles) west of London; 5 kilometres (3 miles) south of Oxford.
Visitor attractions:	Attractive and peaceful riverside; Sandford Lock and Weir; Nuneham House; Radley College and village; woods near Radley.
Start/Finish:	In front of The Tandem pub on Kennington Road (in the middle of Kennington). OS Explorer map 180, GR 523025.
Access:	(*by car*) Drive south from Oxford or north from Abingdon to Kennington, and go into the middle of town. Park in the Kennington Health Centre and Social Club car park, opposite The Tandem pub. Cross the road to the pub.
	(*by train*) Take a train from Paddington to Radley. Walk out of the station approach and turn right. Join the walk on the next corner, where the road over the railway joins Church Road.
	(*by boat*) Salter Brothers' boats link Sandford Lock with Oxford and Abingdon.
Length:	9 kilometres (5½ miles).
Time:	3 hours.
Refreshments:	The King's Arms at Sandford Lock; the Bowyer Arms near Radley Station; The Tandem in Kennington.
Pathway status:	Pavements; dirt tracks; country paths.

Background

Kennington is little more than a quiet suburb of Oxford, but it has some attractive buildings on its main road and back lanes, as you will see towards the end of the walk. Radley village has no great historical importance either, though its college has a good reputation for sports, especially rowing, and you will see how well it caters for its students as you cross its spacious playing fields. As for the river, this section has associations with the children's books *Alice's Adventures in Wonderland* and *Peter Pan*. This is explained more fully in the text of the walk.

The Walk

To the Sandford Lasher

Walk down to the right of The Tandem pub on to a narrow path between tall hedges. Cross the metal footbridge over the railway, then walk straight ahead across a broad gravel drive to a small footbridge over a stream. This leads to a meadow, where the path goes diagonally right to the river. On the opposite bank, there is a well-appointed house. This is the only riverside dwelling that you will see on either side of the river during this walk, apart from a few houses near Sandford Lock.

Turn right and follow the path beside the river. You are unlikely to meet anyone apart from dog walkers and other ramblers. The houses of Kennington are visible to your right, but they too soon disappear from sight as you make your way along a string of islands to Sandford Lock.

When you reach a metal bridge across a backwater of the Thames, turn left and cross it on to an island known as Fiddler's Elbow. Follow the path down the island. Notice the lush vegetation on both banks as you go, and look out for moorhens on their nests in the reeds. Soon you will notice a sizeable property on the opposite bank. This is the Four Pillars Hotel, which has a small landing stage. Here, the path crosses a wooden footbridge and a narrow footpath goes right, leading to Sandford Weir and Pool. This treacherous weir, known as the Sandford Lasher, has claimed the lives of several people, including that of Michael Llewellyn Davies in 1921. He was an undergraduate of Christ Church College in Oxford, and a ward of J. M. Barrie (1860–1937), who in 1904 had written *Peter Pan* for him and his brother. In the 19th century, other boys from Christ Church met a similar fate at the same spot.

The Thames Path itself presents no dangers. Just beyond the wooden footbridge it crosses a small weir before arriving at Sandford Lock (***travellers by boat*** join here). Where Sandford Mill once stood, modern apartments, which are built in the shape of a mill, now enjoy views over the river and the sound of running water beneath the building. You can cross the lock to the Kings Arms, a popular spot at lunchtime with a large garden overlooking the lock.

Nuneham – a Village Removed

On leaving Sandford Lock, cross a bridge over the backwater and turn left to continue along the Thames Path. For the next 2.5 kilometres (1½ miles), until the route leaves the river, there are no towns or villages in sight and you are once more in the company of swans, moorhens and grebes. The river provides all they need – reeds and sedges for their nests, and plenty of weeds to eat. Thick bushes often block your view, but here and there you may notice paths trampled by the birds as they enter and leave the river.

On the horizon ahead you will now see hills, which force the river in a long bend to the right towards Abingdon. This is the only part of its course where it flows westwards. High on the hill you can see Nuneham House, and on its left, a curious domed building with huge columns. This is All Saints Church. The house and church were built for the first Earl of Harcourt in 1756, who had tired of his home

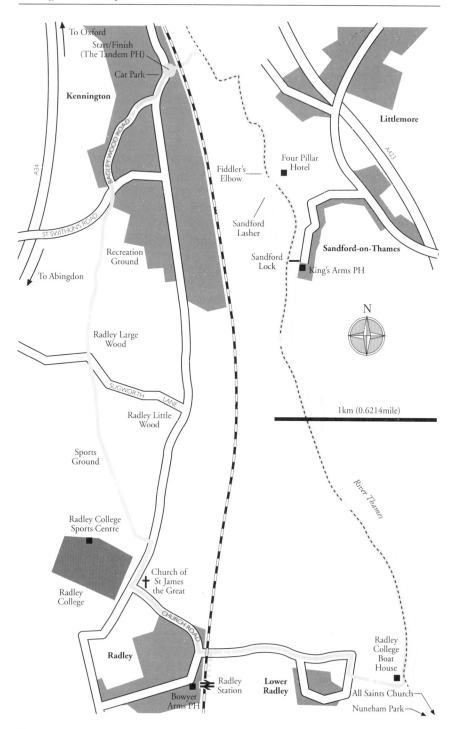

To Oxford

Start/Finish
(The Tandem PH)

Car Park

Kennington

RAGLEY WOOD ROAD

A34

ST SWITHUN'S ROAD

To Abingdon

Recreation
Ground

Radley Large
Wood

SUGWORTH LANE

Radley Little
Wood

Sports
Ground

Radley College
Sports Centre

Radley
College

Church of
St James
the Great

CHURCH ROAD

Radley

Bowyer
Arms PH

Radley
Station

Fiddler's
Elbow

Sandford
Lasher

Sandford
Lock

Four Pillar
Hotel

Littlemore

A423

Sandford-on-Thames

King's Arms PH

N

1km (0.6214mile)

River Thames

**Lower
Radley**

Radley
College
Boat
House

All Saints Church

Nuneham Park

in Stanton Harcourt. There was once a village nearby, but the Earl felt that it spoiled his view; so he had the entire community removed from his sight to a location on the Dorchester Road. In 1840, the house became famous when Queen Victoria and Prince Albert spent their honeymoon there.

This area was a popular destination for people from Oxford in Victorian days, especially in summer, as described by D. MacColl in *The Royal River*:

'The river is as populous as ever then with dashing young fellows in flannel, and enchanting young ladies dressed in the depth of fashion. Great and many barges are towed down to Nuneham, and there merry people dance round Carfax, and float up again to Salter's in the heavy purple dusk, trolling snatches of songs.'

The 'Carfax' referred to is the Carfax Conduit, which was brought here from Oxford for use as a garden ornament.

Charles Dodgson, alias Lewis Carroll, was one of those who enjoyed rowing down this way from Oxford. The Pool of Tears episode in *Alice's Adventures in Wonderland* may well have been inspired by an outing here on a rainy June day in 1862, which he recorded in his diary. His favourite spot was Lock Wood, just beyond Nuneham, which lies out of sight around the bend.

Through Lower and Upper Radley

This walk actually leaves the river just before Nuneham, at the Radley College Boathouse. This private school is the most important feature of the village of Radley, and its reputation for rowing is high indeed. If there is a crew out on the river, you may be able to judge this for yourself. Once past the boathouse, turn right and walk along a sealed drive to a junction. Turn right again, then left at the next junction. From here go straight through Lower Radley, where there are only a few cottages, then between open fields and on again until you pass between more houses.

You are now entering Upper Radley, which is bigger than Lower Radley, but still of no great size. The road slopes up and over the railway, then comes to a junction. If you are in need of refreshment at this point, the Bowyer Arms is just along to the left. (*Travellers by rail* join the walk here – turn right out of the station approach and go straight ahead.) Turn right on to Church Road and walk past a couple of shops. Follow the road round to the left, past a cemetery and up to a junction by a church on the right. This is the church of St James the Great, built in the 15th century. It has a sundial and gargoyles attached to the tower. Inside, there are some impressive stained glass windows and a former Speaker's Chair from the House of Commons, but unfortunately the doors are often locked.

At the junction, cross the road and turn right. Walk past Radley College Sports Centre and a bus stop, then turn left through a kissing gate on to a broad grass path. Go through another kissing gate into the grounds of Radley College and around to the right of playing fields. This will then take you to the left and up a grassy bank, where you will see a running track and football pitch on your left. Turn right with the line of trees and then head to the left of a concrete shelter on the far side of the large playing field (unless a game is in progress, in which case skirt round to the right). Follow the tree line along to the left and look for a gap that leads through to an open field. There are tracks leading into a wood before this, but they do not join up with this route.

Through Fields and Woods to Kennington

Once through the gap, walk along the path with a field to your left and Radley Little Wood to your right. Soon the wood is left behind. Pass telegraph poles and a hedge to your right, then continue across the middle of the field to a gap in the hedge ahead. Cross the narrow lane, called Sugworth Lane, and go straight ahead over a stile. Here, a stone marker indicates the footpath to Kennington.

You are now entering Radley Large Wood. The path keeps to the fringe of the wood, with open fields visible to your left most of the way, but you do pass under dense trees. Although other paths join from the left and right, ignore them and walk straight ahead. Towards the end of the wood, the path goes downhill. Cross some planks over a stream, then bear right and cross a stile into an open area. Walk up a grassy slope with woodland on your left. When you reach the top of the slope, you will see the houses of Kennington to your right.

Go through a kissing gate in the top left-hand corner of the open area. This is a memorial field, dedicated to six locals who lost their lives in World War II. Go on past a cricket pitch, keeping to the left. From here, you might spot a few tower blocks of Oxford over the rooftops of Kennington, reminding you how close you are to the city. Leave the cricket pitch through a wooden barrier in the top corner, and go down a path between houses. Where the path meets a drive, turn left to St Swithun's Road. Cross over into Bagley Wood Road and walk along this quiet, undulating, narrow lane for about a kilometre (½ mile). It comes out in front of St Swithun's Church, where there is a war memorial on the right. Turn left along Kennington Road passing some pretty thatched cottages as you walk the last stretch to the car park.

Abingdon

Summary: This walk has plenty of interesting features as it follows the Thames southward, eastward, and, rather unusually, westward. You pass two places where the river's original course has been altered, and stroll through a quiet, well-preserved village. The route also includes a cross-country ramble through farmland before rejoining the river, and finally passes the grounds of the former abbey and centre of Abingdon town.

Location:	102 kilometres (64 miles) west of London; 10 kilometres (6 miles) south of Oxford.
Start/Finish:	At the meadow on the southwest side of Abingdon Bridge. OS Explorer map 170, GR 499968.
Visitor attractions:	Peaceful riverside meadows; Sutton Pools; Sutton Courtenay village; Swift Ditch; site of former abbey in Abingdon.
Access:	(*by car*) Park in one of the Pay & Display car parks on either side of the A415, just before Abingdon Bridge if you approach from the south. Walk down to the riverside to the west of the bridge.
	(*by bus*) Take the X3 from Oxford (Oxford Bus Company). Walk down Bridge Street to the river, cross the bridge and turn right.
	(*by boat*) Salter Brothers' boats link Abingdon with Oxford.
Length:	11 kilometres (7 miles).
Time:	3½ hours.
Refreshments:	The George & Dragon and The Fish pubs in Sutton Courtenay; Wagon & Horses near Culham; many pubs and restaurants in Abingdon, including The Mill House on Nags Head Island.
Pathway status:	Towpath; pavements; country lanes; narrow tracks.
Best time to visit:	There is a market in Abingdon on Mondays.

Background

The river's route past the town of Abingdon may appear natural enough, but until the late 18th century, the main channel ran through what is known as the Swift Ditch, to the south of town. In the early 19th century another change was made, when the Culham Cut was dug. This left Sutton Pools as a picturesque backwater, and cut off the village of Sutton Courtenay from the river's main route. Sutton Courtenay is a quaint village with many brick and timber houses. In the cemetery of All Saints Church are the graves of a former Prime Minister, Herbert Asquith, and the writer Eric Blair, better known as George Orwell.

The Walk

Across the Swift Ditch

You start the walk on Andersey Island, facing Abingdon. This meadow is a popular place for locals to relax with the papers, walk the dog or feed the ducks and swans, so you may have company at first. The bridge that spans the river here dates back to 1416, though it has been altered considerably since. John Leland, library keeper to Henry VIII, commented of its construction that 'Every man had a penny a day, which was the best wages, and an extraordinary price in those times.'

Turn left and stroll along the river's edge. On the bank beside you are tall, stately trees, while opposite are buildings ranging from ancient to modern, including the massive, tapered spire of St Helen's Church. This spire will remain in sight for much of the walk ahead, and will help you gauge how close you are to town on the return leg.

Just beyond the church, on the opposite bank, there is a small bridge over the Wilts & Berks Canal, dated 1824. The canal is no longer used, but river birds like to congregate at the bridge in the hope of being fed by passers-by. As the path veers south with the river, the view on the left opens up across the low-lying meadow; the opposite bank is lined with the modern housing of suburban Abingdon. The route becomes increasingly peaceful, and discarded feathers on the banks show that this is a favourite resting spot for ducks and geese.

Soon you have left Abingdon behind and are out in open country. You can, however, see the cooling towers of Didcot Power Station straight ahead, and electric pylons that unfortunately are never far from you along this route. The river bends to the left and then to the right, opening up a fine view down Culham Reach.

As you cross a footbridge over a stream on the right bend, notice a fine old bridge to your left, half-concealed by trees and shrubs. The size of the bridge, built at the same time as Abingdon Bridge, suggests that this stream was once larger; and this is in fact the case. You are crossing the Swift Ditch, marked on Ordnance Survey maps simply as Back Water, which was once the main channel of the Thames. The monks at Abingdon Abbey probably diverted part of the river through the town as early as the 10th century, but the Swift Ditch remained the more forceful channel. In 1639, one of the first pound locks along the Thames was built on it, as you will see when you cross it again later. It was only in 1790, when local businessmen instigated the construction of a lock and weir at Abingdon, that boat traffic changed to its present course.

Over Sutton Pools

Continue along the path beside Culham Reach, where willows and alders grow on the bank and the river rolls placidly by. On the left is a large open field, behind which you can see the rooftops and church tower of Culham village. At the end of the reach, the path turns left to follow Culham Cut. Most of the river's flow disappears behind the island created by the cut, but you will meet these waters again shortly at Sutton Pools.

The path climbs the bastion of a former bridge over the cut, giving a brief view of Culham Manor across the field to the left. Continue to the next complete footbridge over the cut and turn right to cross the channel. Follow the path diagonally right across a field and then proceed over several sets of weir gates across Sutton Pools. This is a wonderful area of willows and still waters, with ducks swimming among the lily pads. Continue to the end of the pools, where a few houses backing on to the stream are the start of the village of Sutton Courtenay. Turn right over a small bridge. Here, you can see water flowing on under a high wall, beyond which is the site of a former mill.

Go through a kissing gate on to the main road of Sutton Courtenay. Cross over and go right, passing green verges and attractive houses. Just past the George & Dragon pub is All Saints Church, originally built in the 12th century. At the far end of the graveyard, behind the church, lie the remains of two men who did much to influence 20th-century English society. One is Herbert Asquith (1852–1928), Prime Minister during the last Liberal Government from 1908–16, who laid the foundation for the Welfare State. The other is Eric Blair, better known as George Orwell, whose political satires such as *Animal Farm* and *1984* made him one of the most popular English writers of the 20th century. He died in 1950 at the age of 47, and two rose bushes – one white and the other red – mark his grave.

If you visit the graveyard, leave by the side entrance and turn left. If not, turn left just beyond the church into a narrow alley and walk to the end of the graveyard, then turn left again into All Saints Lane. At the end of the lane, cross the road beside The Fish pub and go straight ahead into a broad sealed drive, which bends to the right. At the end of the drive, go over a stile and along the left side of a field towards Sutton Bridge. Soon the stream from Sutton Pools re-emerges beside you. About 50 metres (55 yards) before you reach the bridge, go through a gate to the right and on to the road. Cross with care to the pavement on the other side.

Round Warren Farm

Turn left over Sutton Bridge and on over Culham Bridge, enjoying views up and downstream. Beyond the bridges, which are connected, cross back to the left just beyond Culham Lock. Walk on past the end of Culham High Street and up to the traffic lights at the junction with the busy main road (A415). Cross over to the Wagon & Horses pub, which is your last chance for refreshment before Abingdon. Cross again to the north side of the road and turn right. After 150 metres (165 yards), turn left into Thame Lane, opposite a signpost for the European School.

There are a few modern houses at the beginning of this lane, but once you pass the school you are out into open countryside. From here your route lies straight ahead for about 1.5 kilometres (1 mile), first along a sealed road and then along a gravel drive, until you reach a bridge over the railway. You pass Warren Farm on the left and are surrounded by fields and pylons. If you look diagonally to the right, you will notice two smooth, rounded hills on the horizon, with clumps of trees on top. These are the Wittenham Clumps, site of an Iron Age hill fort, which are on the route of the next walk.

Just before a brick railway bridge, branch left on to a gravel drive. This skirts the right side of a field, where you can see the railway in a cutting to the right below. The gravel drive climbs, then dips, then disappears altogether, but keep to the right of the field and go over a stile. Here, you can see the buildings of Warren Farm to the left. Beyond, look for the distant spire of St Helen's in Abingdon, and down in front of you, the welcoming sight of the Thames.

Return to the Abbey

Once over the stile, follow a narrow path between fences and descend a steep bank. Cross another stile and head diagonally left to the river, then continue downstream. After 1 kilometre or so (almost a mile), the path bends away from the river to the left, then plunges right, into the undergrowth. Cross a tiny footbridge, then a bigger one that goes over a shallow cascade. This is the beginning of the Swift Ditch that you crossed earlier. As you emerge from the hawthorns on the other side, a plaque on the left explains that this was the site of one of the first pound locks on the Thames.

Turn left and cross a small meadow to a wider bridge over another channel of the Swift Ditch. Follow the path to the right, and it brings you out by the Thames again. The sight of St Helen's spire shows that you are now close to town, and after a couple more bends the path reaches Abingdon Lock. Cross the lock and weir and walk into town with Abbey Stream on your right. Ignore a signpost for the Thames Path and go straight on, with a small golf course on your left and the shallow stream on your right.

Pass some public conveniences and turn right over the footbridge beyond, then go straight ahead into Abbey Gardens. Go left to the statue of Queen Victoria, beside which there is a plaque showing the site of the former abbey. Abingdon Abbey was founded in the 7th century, and by the 10th century, it was an important centre from which the rules of St Benedict were spread to other monasteries in Winchester, Peterborough and Ely. Eventually it was razed after the Dissolution of the Monasteries (1536), and today the only buildings that remain are the Checker (once the treasury), the Checker Hall, now used as a theatre, and the Long Gallery, all of which date from the 13th to 15th centuries. These can be seen off Thames Street at the end of the walk.

If you wander through the dense trees to the left of the statue, you will find a 19th-century folly, overgrown with ivy. Go back to the statue and walk beyond it into a circular garden of flower beds, particularly colourful in summer. Leave this by a pathway to the left, turn right and go through a large, ancient gateway into the centre of town.

Just beyond the Abbey Gateway, you will see a plaque on the left stating that John Foysse opened a school here in 1563. On the right is St Nicholas Church, which dates back to the 12th century. Opposite the gateway, supported on columns, is the County Hall, which looks out over the Market Place. The ground floor of the building, constructed in 1678–82, is used as a covered market, while the first floor, formerly a courtroom, now houses Abingdon's museum.

Turn left down Bridge Road. You will pass two pubs on your left, the Crown and

Thistle and the Broad Face, and the Tourist Information Office on your right. Turn left along Thames Street beside the Broad Face if you want to look at the abbey ruins, turning left again into an alley near the end of the street (see Opening Times). Alternatively, continue over the bridge. Go past the Mill House, a pub and restaurant in the middle of the river on Nags Head Island, and on to the car park.

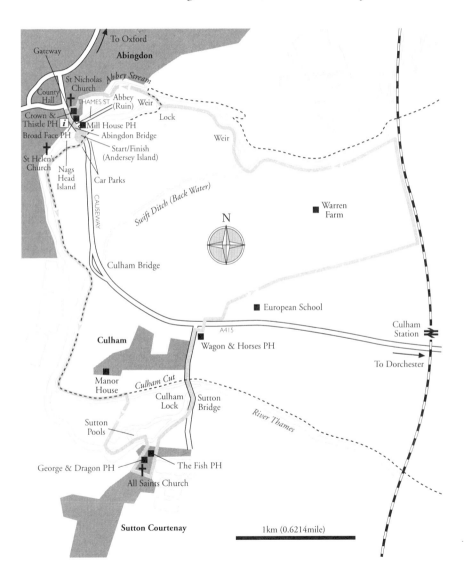

Wittenham Clumps

Summary: This stroll through English history begins with a climb up the symmetrical domes of the Wittenham Clumps, where clear traces of an Iron Age fort still exist along with an intriguing 'poem tree'. It then wanders down through Little Wittenham Wood and across fields to Shillingford. After crossing the river, it winds through the back alleys of Shillingford and along a short stretch of main road before leading down to the riverside. Once the tiny River Thame has joined the Thames, the path goes inland to explore Dorchester Abbey (option) and the Dyke Hills, which once enclosed a large town. It then returns to the river, and crosses back to Little Wittenham via a bridge just below Day's Lock. Pendon Museum (see page 74) is conveniently located for this walk, if you have time.

Location:	96 kilometres (60 miles) west of London; 6.5 kilometres (4 miles) southeast of Abingdon.
Start/Finish:	In front of St Peter's Church in Little Wittenham. OS Explorer map 170, GR 566935.
Visitor attractions:	Iron Age fort; panoramic views; woodland walk; ancient dykes; Dorchester Abbey (option).
Access:	(*by car*) From the northwest corner of Wallingford, take the A4130 towards Didcot, then the first right towards the Wittenhams. Take the first right again and follow this into Little Wittenham village, ignoring a left turn at the beginning of the village. Park in front of St Peter's Church.
	(*by bus*) Take bus 105 (Stagecoach Oxford) from Oxford to Dorchester. Walk to the south end of town, passing (or visiting – see option) the abbey on the left, and branch right down Bridge End. Pass a church on the left, then bear right and go down Wittenham Lane. Continue beside a field. When you reach the line of earth ramparts, turn right and join the walk at Dyke Hills.
Length:	9.5 kilometres (6 miles).
Time:	3 hours.
Refreshments:	Shillingford Bridge Hotel; the Kingfisher and The Old Bell pubs (also in Shillingford); the George Inn and White Hart pubs in Dorchester.
Pathway status:	Pavements; country paths; farm tracks.

Background

Although sparsely populated these days, this was once a busy area, as evidenced by the fortifications on Castle Hill and the lines of dykes across the river to the north. Two of the main reasons for this were its rich farmland and the far-reaching view from the

Plate 8: *The Trout Inn, with its view of Godstow Weir, resident peacocks and low-beamed interior, is a popular Thames-side tavern (see page 46).*

Plate 9: *A solitary riverside residence in the quiet Oxford suburb of Kennington (see page 52).*

Plate 10: *An impressive view of Nuneham House, with a rape field in bloom and pollarded willows by the Thames. In 1840, Queen Victoria and Prince Albert spent their honeymoon here (see page 52).*

Plate 11: *Bridge over the Wilts & Berks Canal where it joins the Thames in Abingdon (see page 58).*

Plate 12: *Bright flower beds in Abingdon Abbey Gardens (see page 60).*

Plate 13: *Panoramic view from Wittenham Clumps, showing the Thames and Day's Lock (see page 62).*

Plate 14: *Pleasure boat moored beside the Swan Diplomat Hotel at Streatley (see page 74).*

Plate 15: *Stately riverside houses are a common sight on the Streatley walk (see page 78).*

hill. In the late Iron Age, when tribes gradually stopped warring, hill forts were abandoned in favour of lowland communities – for example, in the area enclosed between the dykes and the river near Dorchester. Later, the Romans established the town of Durocina, now Dorchester, which the Saxons developed into a missionary centre for the south of England.

Dorchester Abbey (see option, page 69) is one of the great ecclesiastical centres in England. In the 10th century, the town was at the centre of a diocese that stretched up to the Humber. The Normans moved the bishopric to Lincoln in the early 12th century, and an Augustinian Abbey was founded on the site of a former cathedral. Coaching inns on the main road reflect a time when travellers would stop here on their journey between London and Oxford.

The Walk

Back to the Iron Age

Go through the gate opposite the church in Little Wittenham and into Little Wittenham Nature Reserve. Before beginning the climb, pause to appreciate the symmetry of Round Hill, with its tuft of trees above the smooth slopes. Follow the path along the right-hand edge of the first field, then go straight up a broad path to the top. Beware – it is steeper than it looks! It is easy to see how difficult the hill would have been to assault, as the entire perimeter is exposed. The panoramic view from the top, which includes the Thames winding past Day's Lock and an endless patchwork of fields, is a rarity in the flat landscapes of southern England.

Go to the right around the top of the hill. Here, a similar panorama unfolds, though on this side the massive towers of Didcot Power Station stand out to the west. Follow a path heading down the hill towards a car park, but cut across left on another path before you reach it. This leads up to the second of the Wittenham Clumps – Castle Hill. At the start of the short climb, you pass over a causeway above a deep ditch. This is the first sign of the Iron Age fort that once occupied the site. At the top of the slope lies an uneven plateau, on which archaeologists have found evidence of round houses and grain stores.

Follow the path into the woods, and keep on the main track as it climbs gently. Where it levels out, take a right fork beneath huge beech trees. This leads into a restful dell beside the fringe of the wood. In 1844, a certain Joseph Tubb inscribed a poem on the smooth bark of a large beech tree at the edge of the dell. Follow the path leading out to the left to see the tree, which is now dead. It is difficult to make out the words on the bark these days, but a plaque just outside the clump of trees recounts the poem for us:

> *As up the hill with labouring sticks we tread,*
> *Where the twin clumps their sheltering branches spread,*
> *The summit gained, at ease reclining lay*
> *And all around the widespread scene survey.*

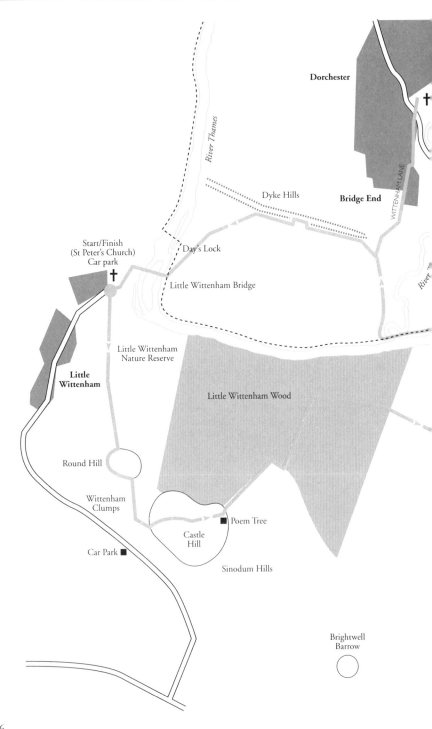

Dorchester

River Thames

Dyke Hills

Bridge End

WITTENHAM LANE

Day's Lock

Start/Finish
(St Peter's Church)
Car park

Little Wittenham Bridge

River

Little Wittenham
Nature Reserve

**Little
Wittenham**

Little Wittenham Wood

Round Hill

Wittenham
Clumps

Poem Tree

Castle
Hill

Car Park ■

Sinodum Hills

Brightwell
Barrow

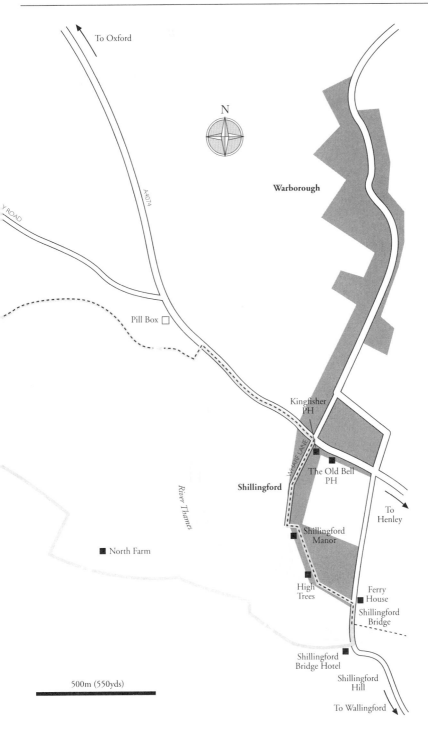

Tubb goes on to describe features in the surrounding landscape, many of which remain unchanged today. Dorchester Abbey is clearly visible to the north, and Brightwell Barrow, about the same height as Castle Hill, can be seen to the south-east. Take a good look at this scene, for your route now lies downhill.

Down Through Little Wittenham Wood

Follow the path that leads down towards the left-hand corner of the field, crossing another causeway and deep ditch. Go over a stile and down the left side of a field. At the bottom, turn right for a few steps, then go left through a barred gate into Little Wittenham Wood. The track slopes gently downward through a variety of trees – ash, beech, oak, and pines planted in rows.

Pass a wooden barrier, then turn right at a junction with a broad path. From here the track is flat, and all too soon emerges from the woodland to continue across fields towards Shillingford. As you walk along the left edge of a large field, the Thames lies out of sight to your left. Beyond the woods, Castle Hill becomes visible again over your right shoulder, along with Brightwell Barrow, capped by two solitary trees. Keep going until you reach a barred gate leading to farm buildings, then turn right.

At the end of the first field, turn left and follow a broad track between two electrified fences. Pass the farmhouse and carry on until you meet its driveway. Cross this and bear slightly right, passing a barred gate, and go along an avenue of ash and hawthorn. The river comes into view along here, as well as a grand property on the opposite bank. The path then branches right through a gate about 20 metres (22 yards) before the river.

Walk through the gate and under a large oak tree towards a fenced-off field, which the path follows round to the left. When you reach a gate in the field, go through it and diagonally right across the field to another gate. Turn left and walk down a broad path into the car park of the Shillingford Bridge Hotel, beside Shillingford Bridge. This fine balustraded stone bridge was built in 1827 and offers good views both up- and downstream. Cross the bridge, keeping an eye on the traffic, as there is no pavement here. Carry on for about 50 metres (55 yards), then turn left into the private road opposite Ferry House. When this bends left by a house called High Trees, turn right through a kissing gate and into a narrow alley, signposted Thames Path.

To the Dykes and Dorchester

Little can be seen along this alley due to high walls and fences. Cross the broad entrance to Shillingford Manor and carry on until another path emerges from the left, by a metal barrier. Turn down this path, walk past a wooden thatched building and out on to a road. As you emerge from the alley, look on the wall of an old house to the left. You will find plaques recording the level of devastating floods in the past – some of them above head height.

Here the Thames is just on your left, but another detour is necessary before you can walk beside it. Turn right up Wharf Lane, away from the river, and go up to the junction with the main road (A4074) beside the Kingfisher pub (The Old Bell is along the main road to the right). Cross the road with care, turn left and walk beside the main road for about 500 metres (550 yards). When you reach a sign to Dorchester on your right, cross back over the road, go through a kissing gate and walk down to the Thames, visited rather late on this walk to avoid a climb at the end of the route.

Turn right and walk upstream. Look out for a pill box (see page 36) in the far corner of the field. Carry on into the second field, then follow the banks, thick with wildflowers and reeds, as far as a wooden footbridge. To the left you can see Wittenham Clumps, which get nearer as you approach the end of the walk, while to the right are the rooftops of Dorchester and the abbey itself. Cross a small foot-bridge, which spans the confluence of the Thames with the tiny Thame. Then, instead of following the riverbank, turn right, walking away from the river, and go through a kissing gate.

Keep going straight until you see a double line of raised earthworks on your left. At this point, you can turn left to pass through the dykes and return to Little Wittenham, or go straight ahead to visit Dorchester and its abbey. For Dorchester, keep walking towards the houses ahead, past a pill box and along the right side of a field. Continue along Wittenham Lane, then branch right and keep heading north along Bridge End. This joins the main road, and the abbey is just up on the right.

Option – Dorchester Abbey

The abbey was built in the 12th century, but considerably enlarged over the following two centuries. One of its finest features is the detailed tracery (ornamental stone work) over the windows in the chancel, in particular the Jesse window in the north of the chancel. This tells the story of Christianity from the time of Jesse, who was the father of King David and an ancestor of Christ.

Dorchester owes its fame to St Birinus, who was largely responsible for the spread of Christianity through southern England in the 7th century. If history had happened a little differently, Dorchester might now be the nation's capital. Its current inhabitants are probably glad this is not the case, since the medieval town with its cosy, timber-framed and thatched cottages is generally left in peace.

Across the Dykes and the River

Retrace your steps to the Dyke Hills (**walkers arriving by bus** join here). Climb the line of dykes nearest the river and walk westwards along them. It is obvious that they must have taken considerable manpower to construct, and were therefore used to protect a big and important community. Between them and the river there is now nothing but fields, but this site of over 40 hectares (100 acres) was once densely inhabited by late Iron Age people. Archaeologists have discovered a grid layout and many coins buried in the ground. From where you are standing, you can trace the movement of people through history – from the fort on Castle Hill, down to the protected lowlands and, finally, under Roman influence, into the area where Dorchester now stands.

At the end of the first dyke, walk through a gate into a field where lower dykes border a similar channel. These were once ploughed to make the ground better for grazing, a process that unearthed the skeletons of a Saxon man and woman. This showed that the site continued to be inhabited after Roman times. At the end of the second field, go through a gate and turn left along a narrow path between fields. Where this path ends, go diagonally right across a field to a white iron bridge that leads over the Thames.

Cross this bridge, which is situated just downstream from Day's Lock, and walk past the lock-keeper's house on a small island. The name of the lock here shows that locks were once privately owned, the lock keeper taking a toll from all who passed through. Most locks have now reverted to the name of their location, though there are still some, like this one, far from any town or village, that retain an owner's name from days gone by.

Cross a second and third bridge, then follow a sealed path round to the left, up a slope, then round to the right. You now find yourself in front of St Peter's Church in Little Wittenham.

Wallingford

Summary: This walk is short and sweet – ideal for a day when you want some fresh air but don't want to go too far. However, if it is combined with an exploration of the town and/or nearby Pendon Museum (option), it could occupy a full day. Wallingford was one of the earliest towns to appear on the banks of the Thames and now seems frozen in the past, its narrow streets forming a living museum. The walk goes round the castle ruins, then sets off across fields to Benson Lock and finally returns to Wallingford along a lovely stretch of the Thames Path.

Location:	91 kilometres (57 miles) west of London; 16 kilometres (10 miles) south of Oxford.
Start/Finish:	Entrance to the castle grounds on Castle Street (A329) near junction with High Street. OS Explorer map170, GR 607896.
Visitor attractions:	Narrow streets of Wallingford; Wallingford Museum; Saxon ramparts; castle ruins; riverside views; Benson Lock; Pendon Museum (option).
Access:	(*by car*) From Wallingford Bridge, go west along the High Street. After the traffic light in the centre of town, turn right into Castle Street and park in the Pay & Display car park on the right. The entrance to the castle grounds is just beyond the car park.
	(*by bus*) Take the 39 bus (Stagecoach Oxford) from Oxford to Wallingford. Walk north along St Martin's Street to the High Street, then cross straight over into Castle Street. Walk 100 metres (110 yards) and the entrance to Castle Gardens is on the right.
Length:	5 kilometres (3 miles).
Time:	1½ hours.
Refreshments:	Several pubs and restaurants in Wallingford; tea at the Riverside Café beyond Benson Lock.
Path status:	Pavements; farm tracks; country paths.
Best time to visit:	Friday for the weekly market. Saturday or Sunday for Pendon Museum.

Background

As its name suggests, Wallingford developed around a ford. In the days before bridges, this ford offered the most convenient crossing of the Thames above London. The first recorded bridge here dates from 1141. The grid patterns of the streets suggest that the town was laid out by the Romans. It then became a major Saxon stronghold, fortified by ramparts that are some of the best surviving examples in England today. The easiest place to view them is opposite the museum on the Kine Croft. The museum itself, located in the 15th-century timber-framed Flint House on the High Street, is probably the best place to begin an exploration of the town. For railway enthusiasts, steam trains occasionally run on the Wallingford–Cholsey branch line.

William the Conqueror came here in 1067 and immediately ordered a grand castle to be built, which was completed in 1071. In 1154, Henry II secured the throne through the Treaty of Wallingford, and in 1155 he gave the town its charter to establish guilds and hold regular markets. To this day it remains a market town, with a weekly market on Fridays.

The narrow streets are packed with ancient buildings. The 17th-century Town Hall stands at the end of Market Place, supported on Doric pillars, and to its left is the Corn Exchange (1856), which now functions as a theatre and cinema. There are two churches of note near the river. The oldest is St Leonard's, in the southeast corner of town, a typical Norman structure. However, the most striking is St Peter's, which, although now unused, is still Wallingford's most prominent landmark. When it was completed in 1777, the unconventional design of its tall, slender spire caused quite a stir.

St Peter's was the brainchild of Sir William Blackstone (1723–80), a judge who is best remembered for his *Commentaries on the Laws of England*. This document had an influence on the drafting of the American Declaration of Independence. Sir William is buried in the grounds of St Peter's. Another famous local was Agatha Christie (1890–1976), who spent 35 years at Winterbrook Lodge and is buried in nearby Cholsey Church. It is strange to think that her stories, full of murder and intrigue, were written in the peaceful and pastoral environment of Wallingford.

The Walk

Round the Castle Remains

Walk down the path beside a small cemetery and enter the castle grounds through a gateway on the left (closed during bad weather in winter). The gardens are meticulously laid out with flower beds, a fountain and towering pines, and have won awards for their beauty. Follow the path straight ahead and go up the steps of the mound where the castle once stood. From here, there is a fine view across the gardens below. The largest remnant of the castle, known as St Nicholas' College, stands in the southeast corner of the mound, and is thought to be a small part of the king's chapel.

Cross the small wooden bridge to the north of the castle ruins. Follow the spiral path to the summit of a high mound, or 'motte', where a wooden tower once stood. At the top, you can look across the rooftops of the town and catch glimpses of the river. In the field to the north, you can also see more fragments of the castle, giving an idea of its original size. From the 11th to the 17th century, it gave the town enormous significance, and must have been an awesome sight. The antiquary William Camden (1551–1623) commented that 'its size and magnificence used to strike me with amazement, when I came thither a lad from Oxford'. During the

Civil War, it was the last defence of Royalist troops, who held out here for several months before surrendering to Cromwell's troops. Cromwell himself ordered its destruction in 1652.

On to Benson Lock

Retrace your steps to the castle grounds entrance, cross Castle Street (A329) and turn right. Follow the road past a huge gateway (part of the castle), then round a bend to the right and another to the left. You are now out of town; from here on, fields border the road. When you see a public footpath sign on the opposite side of the road, just beyond a small gatehouse and flint wall, cross over and go down a wide sealed drive between two cemeteries. The one on the left is new, trim and well kept, but the old one on the right is even more attractive. It has some enormous fir trees in its grounds, along with mid-19th-century twin chapels. These unpretentious, graceful structures are built out of flint, and decorated with carved figures.

Continue down the lane beyond the cemeteries as it becomes a farm track. Just before a bend to the left, look to the right, where you can see fragments of the castle in the field and the prominent spire of St Peter's. A planted field slopes up on your left and a meadow dotted with pines dips away towards the river on your right. The track ends at a barred metal gate. Go through a kissing gate beside it and into a field. You may spot the tops of boats passing along the Thames, which is just across the field ahead.

Instead of continuing on to the river, turn left and walk along the boundary of two fields, where the path is not clearly defined. (If the fields are very boggy, you can go straight ahead from the kissing gate to the Thames Path, then left to Benson Lock.) On the left, the field is bordered by a profusion of bushes and trees, including alder, ash, hawthorns and poplars. At the end of the second field, turn right and walk along its perimeter to a stile in the corner. Once over the stile, you are on the Thames Path, looking across at an island with a well-kept lawn and a backstream appearing from behind it.

Turn left towards Benson Lock, following the path as it swings to the left, a sign of recent erosion. Just before you turn right into the lock grounds, there is a pill box (see page 36) in the field on the left, overgrown with shrubs and lichen. Cross the lower lock gates and continue over the wide weir to a wooden bridge. The little stream passing beneath it has reeds and weeds swaying on its surface, and flows on under a former mill beside the island. If you would like to visit a teashop on the riverfront, continue over this footbridge, turn left, then left again just before the main road. The Riverside Café is on the right by the river.

Wallingford's Ancient Bridge

From the teashop or the footbridge, go back across the weir and lock and rejoin the path, this time heading south. Though much of this route has been chosen for the interest of Wallingford itself, the short walk from Benson to Wallingford also happens to be one of the most attractive stretches of the river. In summer, willowherb, purple loosestrife and vetches grow in profusion along the riverbank, and breaks in the hawthorn bushes allow views of the river. You can also spy a few houses between the

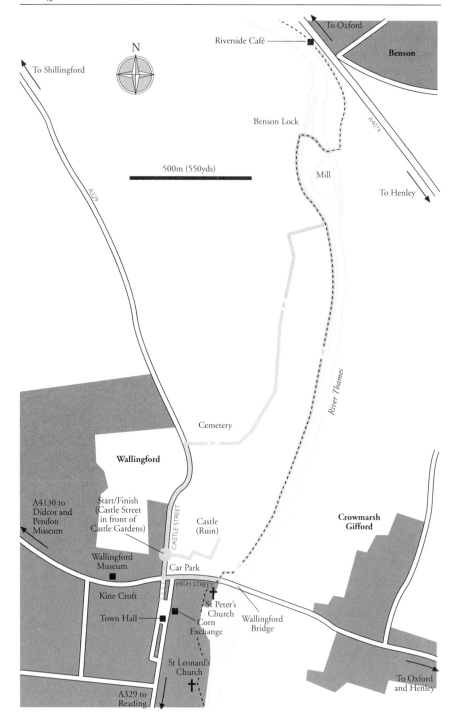

To Shillingford

N

Riverside Café

Benson

500m (550yds)

Benson Lock

A4074

Mill

To Henley

River Thames

A329

Cemetery

Wallingford

A4130 to
Didcot and
Pendon
Museum

Start/Finish
(Castle Street
in front of
Castle Gardens)

CASTLE STREET

Castle
(Ruin)

Crowmarsh
Gifford

Wallingford
Museum

Car Park

Kine Croft

HIGH STREET

St Peter's
Church

Town Hall

Corn
Exchange

Wallingford
Bridge

St Leonard's
Church

A329 to
Reading

To Oxford
and Henley

To Oxford

willows and maples on the opposite side. The river is about 20 metres (22 yards) wide here, with dense rushes on both banks.

As the path approaches Wallingford you come to a kissing gate, opposite a boathouse with a spiral staircase on its side. A little later you cross a small bridge, and pass under tall weeping willows. On the opposite bank is a camping and caravan site. You then come out on an open, grassy area just above Wallingford Bridge, and from this angle you can see most of its great length. It has 17 spans in all, and has needed several reparations in its turbulent history. In 1641, Royalist troops blew up the four central arches and installed a drawbridge to afford the town better protection. Then, in 1809, it was washed away by a tremendous flood. The three central arches that you see today date from the subsequent reconstruction.

Turn right as you approach the bridge and pass between the buildings. You emerge on the High Street with the bridge to your left. Turn right along the High Street until you reach Castle Street, again on the right. Here, you can turn right to go back to the car park, left for the town centre and buses, or go straight ahead to the museum and ramparts.

Option – Pendon Museum

A visit to Pendon is more like observing a work of art in progress than walking around a museum. The aim of the museum is to recapture the beauty and charm of the English countryside as it was around 1930, through miniature reproductions of thatched cottages and scenes of village life. The models are on a scale of 1:76 and the detail is so realistic that the modellers' craft has become an art form. The main exhibit, housed upstairs, is based on villages in the nearby Vale of White Horse. Work has been going on for 40 years and is still far from finished. Downstairs there are exhibits of a railway viaduct on Dartmoor, complete with running trains and passengers, and an imaginary railway scene called Madder Valley. The effect of Pendon is to induce nostalgia for a golden age of rural living, now gone for ever.

To get to Pendon, take the A4130 from Wallingford towards Didcot. After passing turns on the left for Brighton-cum-Sotwell, take a right turn towards the Wittenhams. Ignore the first turning on the right to Little Wittenham, and take the next right; then branch right again at a fork. At Long Wittenham, turn left. The museum is at the end of the village on the right. Pendon is also conveniently situated for walk 10 (Wittenham Clumps), but is included here as this walk is shorter.

Streatley

Summary: This is perhaps the most demanding of all the walks, in that it is longer than the others and involves some climbing. However, it is also very rewarding, beginning with wonderful views of the Thames from Lardon Chase as it flows through the Goring Gap. The route then descends into Streatley and along the Thames Path to Moulsford, where it turns away from the river into rolling hills. It returns via the Ridgeway (one of England's oldest roads) and finishes with a climb across a golf course. Goring, on the opposite bank of the Thames from Streatley, is also well worth exploring. Both towns offer plenty of places to find refreshment after the rigours of the walk.

Location:	87 kilometres (54 miles) west of London; 37 kilometres (23 miles) south of Oxford.
Start/Finish:	Lardon Chase, a National Trust area about 1 kilometre (½ mile) west of Streatley. OS Explorer map 170, GR 583806.
Visitor attractions:	View of Goring Gap; Beetle & Wedge Hotel; walking on the Ridgeway.
Access:	(*by car*) Streatley lies between Reading and Wallingford on the A329. Take the B4009 heading west from the centre of Streatley. Follow up a steep hill and take the first turning on the right at the top of the hill into a free car park.
	(*by train*) Take a train to Reading and then to Goring and Streatley (hourly service). Turn left outside the station, then first left over the railway bridge. This road (the High Street) winds all the way through Goring to the bridge over the river. Cross the bridge, and turn right after just 20 metres (22 yards) into a gravel lane, joining the walk at St Mary's Church.
Length:	14.5 kilometres (9 miles).
Time:	4½ hours
Refreshments:	Moulsford: the Beetle & Wedge Hotel. Streatley: The Bull pub; The Swan Diplomat Hotel. Goring: Riverside Tearooms (by bridge); pubs: the Miller of Mansfield; the John Barleycorn; the Catherine Wheel. Since there are no refreshments available after Moulsford, it is advisable to carry water (and perhaps a packed lunch) on this walk.
Pathway status:	Towpath; pavements; wooded tracks; country lanes and paths.

Background

As with many towns along the Thames, Streatley and Goring came into being because of the local topography – they lie on what was a convenient fording point in the days before bridges. This is the only point on the Thames where two towns of similar size developed facing each other. A rivalry has existed down the ages, partly for territorial reasons. The Thames once divided Wessex and Mercia here, and now divides Berkshire and Oxfordshire.

A hint of the local rivalry can be seen on the Streatley side of the bridge, where Goring's boundary sign clearly claims the river as its own. From the bridge there is a fine view of the weir and lock. Interestingly, there was no bridge until 1837, which helps to explain the rivalry between the towns. Relations could hardly have improved when in 1647, a ferry returning from an annual feast in Goring was swept over the weir. It was overloaded with 60 revellers from Streatley, none of whom survived.

In Goring itself, there are many attractive Georgian and Edwardian buildings, including the curiously-named Miller of Mansfield (Mansfield is in Nottinghamshire). According to legend, this miller served a delicious meal of venison and ale to a passing traveller. However, the deer had been poached from the king, Henry III, who was the traveller in disguise. Instead of punishing the miller, the king gave him land at Goring on the condition that he continued to offer hospitality to travellers. Other buildings of note are Ferry House in Ferry Lane, where Oscar Wilde wrote *An Ideal Husband*, and the Norman church, dedicated to St Thomas of Canterbury, which contains many ancient monuments and brasses, and a bell that is over 600 years old.

The Walk

The Goring Gap

Go to the far left-hand corner of the car park and through a gate. Follow a path with a tall hedge on the left and a sloping field on the right. You are now on Lardon Chase. After about 500 metres (550 yards), the hedge turns a sharp left. From here you can enjoy a view of the Goring Gap, where the Thames passes between the Berkshire Downs and Streatley on the near side, and the Chilterns and Goring on the far side. The church towers of each town rise above trees near the bridge. The river itself is visible just upstream from the bridge and Goring Lock, then again some distance south of the towns as it heads east towards Whitchurch.

After enjoying the view, make your way down the hillside towards a cluster of houses in Streatley (there is no clearly defined path here). Go through a gate in the corner of the field and down a track past the Old Schoolhouse. Turn left at the main road and walk for 200 metres (220 yards) or so. Go straight on at the traffic lights, with The Bull pub on your right. Wells Stores, opposite The Bull, sells a huge selection of cheeses. The road continues on to the river, but you turn left 20 metres (22 yards) before the bridge down a gravel lane, following a signpost to the Thames Path (***visitors arriving by train*** join here).

A Riverside Ramble

The path bends right then left around St Mary's Church. Where it branches, follow the narrow wooded path to the right, marked Thames Path. This veers right, crosses

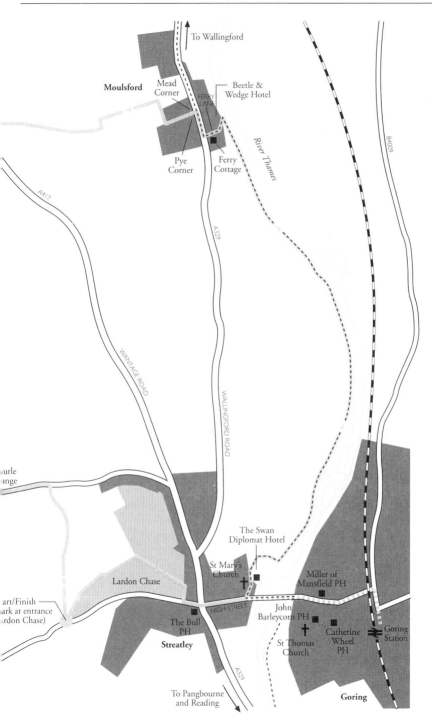

To Wallingford

Moulsford

Mead Corner

Beetle & Wedge Hotel

FERRY LANE

Pye Corner

Ferry Cottage

River Thames

A417

A329

B4009

WANTAGE ROAD

WALLINGFORD ROAD

urle ange

Start/Finish ark at entrance rdon Chase)

Lardon Chase

The Swan Diplomat Hotel

St Mary's Church

The Bull PH

HIGH STREET

Streatley

A329

John Barleycorn PH

St Thomas Church

Miller of Mansfield PH

Catherine Wheel PH

Goring Station

Goring

To Pangbourne and Reading

a small wooden footbridge, goes over a stile and across a meadow to the riverside. Here, turn left and walk upstream. You will see palatial houses and snug boathouses on the opposite bank as the route meanders through open meadows and along tree-lined paths.

The path soon arrives at Cleeve Lock, then continues beside a large field and a comparatively straight stretch of river. Around the last weekend of July this is the site of the annual Streatley and Goring Regatta, when the field is packed with bright funfair attractions. On the opposite bank is a pub, Ye Olde Leatherne Bottel, and the Goring Thames Sailing Club. The river is about 40 metres (44 yards) wide here, and the banks are only 50 centimetres (1.5 feet) above the river itself.

Continue along the riverbank, passing willows, bullrushes and molehills, the kind of landscape that brings to mind *The Wind in the Willows* (Kenneth Grahame, 1908). To the left there is an expansive view of rolling hills, where your route will take you. As you approach Moulsford, go through a kissing gate. Follow the narrow wooded path, then a sealed path to another kissing gate.

Go on into the grounds of the Beetle & Wedge, a classic riverside hotel, immortalized as 'The Potwell Inn' in H.G. Wells' 1910 novel *The History of Mr Polly*. The route leaves the river here, but if you would like to linger, enjoy a drink under the Hotel's signboard. This shows a 'beetle', which was a kind of mallet, once used to drive a wedge into tree trunks and split them into planks so that they could be floated down the river to London. This practice ceased in the 18th century.

Into the Hills

Turn left through the hotel car park and walk up Ferry Lane to the main road (A329). You will pass a high flint wall on the right and the attractive Ferry Cottage on the left. Turn right and walk about 200 metres (220 yards) until you are opposite two pretty cottages, Pye Corner and Mead Corner. Cross the road with care and go up the gravel drive between the cottages. Pass through a gap in a wooden fence into a dead-end street and keep walking, past Meadow Close on the right, until the road bends sharply to the left. Bear right here and follow a dirt track. This soon becomes very narrow, with house gardens on the right and a large open field on the left.

When you see a cricket ground on the right, take a sharp left turn on to a narrow footpath that climbs gently and is sometimes overgrown. When it crosses another path, turn left and go through a gap in the fence. This takes you into a huge open field with pylons in it. Follow the path on the right of the field, which climbs steadily and passes under the electric cables. Keep on this path beside the trees as it bends to the left and then the right. Once around this right-hand corner, a beautiful view of rolling hills opens up. Follow along the right-hand side of this field, where the path levels out and is bordered by elderberry bushes, brambles and teasels on the right.

When the path reaches a main road (A417), cross over, walk a few paces to the right and turn left into a sealed drive leading to Starveall Farm. Follow the drive as it bends left, then right, in front of farm buildings. Continue past a sign marked 'Well Barn Estate – No Thoroughfare' (this warning applies to cars, not walkers). Where the track (now gravel) branches, bear left through tall sycamore trees. You now begin the toughest part of the walk – a long climb with a thick wood (curiously called

Unhill Wood) on the right. It is not particularly steep, but the loose gravel can cause walkers to slip, so walk carefully. As the path climbs higher, the view becomes increasingly interesting. It is worth pausing near the top, both to appreciate the vista and to catch your breath. If you stand quietly, you may well see pheasants, hares or rabbits, too.

Continue on the broad track as it goes down a slope. Where it swings to the left, turn right on to a footpath that takes you to a pretty dell. Where it goes up to the right, branch left down a footpath into a densely-wooded area (the area to the right is marked 'Strictly Private'). The footpath climbs through the wood for a short way, then goes down, and a view opens out across a narrow valley. When you come to a gravel drive, turn right and follow it up into a lovely wooded area of beech and pines. If your legs are beginning to tire at this stage, take heart, for the worst of the climbing is over!

Continue along this drive, ignoring the first lane that joins it from the right. At the second lane, where the drive slopes down to the left, go straight ahead along a signposted footpath and into woodland. The path is on the level from here, passing ferns, rhododendron bushes and stately beech trees, but it can be slippery after rain, so watch your footing.

Along the Ridgeway

When you come to a house on the left, follow the path round to the right. Go over a high stile and down the gravel drive leading away from the farmhouse. After 200 metres (220 yards), take a sharp left on to another gravel track. This is the Ridgeway, an ancient path that has been used for at least 4,000 years, and is now a National Trail. Originally, it ran from Dorset to the North Sea, but the National Trail goes from Wiltshire to Buckinghamshire. In the past, taking this high route was an advantage as it avoided thick woods, marshland, and also the dangerous animals that once inhabited the valleys. The track goes gently downhill with open fields on each side and hawthorns, young oaks and sycamores along the way. It continues in an almost straight line for more than 1.5 kilometre (1 mile).

At the bottom of the long downhill path, Warren Farm lies on the right. It is operated by the Kulika Charitable Trust and offers training in sustainable agriculture for Africa – something of a surprise in this quiet corner of the English countryside. From here the Ridgeway, now sealed and on the level, branches very slightly left. It is open to cars, but few vehicles venture down here. Continue past Thurle Grange, a country mansion on the left. Walk up a slight rise and pass a few houses on the right, then turn right into a short, sealed road with a barn on the left. Go through a gate into a golf course. Follow a footpath sign, bear slightly left at first and then climb straight up the hill to a hedge. Go through an enclosed path and you will find yourself back in the car park.

Pangbourne Meadow

Summary: This walk follows a beautifully isolated stretch of the river, populated mainly by ducks, swans and moles. After a long stroll beside open fields with sweeping views of the Chilterns, the route leaves the river at Mapledurham Lock; it then returns along a narrow track near the railway line, beside a lush stream. Apart from its traffic, the village of Pangbourne is pleasant, and the nearby options of Beale Park and Basildon Park make this an excellent day out.

Location:	77 kilometres (48 miles) west of London; 6.5 kilometres (4 miles) west of Reading.
Start/Finish:	Pangbourne Meadow, beside toll bridge over Thames at Pangbourne. OS Explorer map 171, GR 637767.
Visitor attractions:	Riverside meadows; views of Chilterns; pretty lock; Mapledurham House; village of Pangbourne; Beale Park and Basildon Park (options).
Access:	(*by car*) Pangbourne lies on the A329 just west of Reading. From the middle of the village, take the B471 heading north towards Whitchurch and then turn right just before the toll bridge into River Meadows Pay & Display car park. Walk to the far end of the car park and into Pangbourne Meadow.
	(*by train*) Take the train from Paddington to Pangbourne. Turn right out of the station and go down to Shooter's Hill Road. Turn right, go under the railway bridge and on to a mini-roundabout. Turn left, then left again at the next mini-roundabout. This takes you under the railway again. Follow the road round, and where it begins to rise towards the toll bridge, turn right into the car park and go on into Pangbourne Meadow.
Length:	8 kilometres (5 miles).
Time:	2½ hours.
Refreshments:	Teas are served in summer at Mapledurham Lock; otherwise there are many restaurants, pubs and a tea house in Pangbourne.
Path status:	Country paths; gravel drive; sealed road.

Background

'Bourne' means stream, and in this case it refers to the tiny River Pang, which joins the Thames here. It can be seen flowing under the High Street near the junction with Church Road. The High Street is full of quaint buildings, and the village sign, outside the Village Hall, depicts two local heroes who are separated by over 1,000 years. The first is King Berhtulf, who gave the village its charter in the 9th century, and the second is Kenneth Grahame (1859–1932), author of the children's classic

The Wind in the Willows. Grahame lived in Church Cottage, next to the church of St James the Less, from 1924 until he died.

Mapledurham House, which is glimpsed halfway along this walk, is a beautiful Elizabethan mansion set among riverside meadows. It has its own 14th-century church and 15th-century water mill, which is still working. The house is the setting for the final chapters of John Galsworthy's (1876–1933) *The Forsyte Saga*, and has been used in several film and TV productions.

The Walk

Tales of the Riverbank

The walk begins beside the distinctive, white-painted, iron toll bridge that joins Pangbourne with Whitchurch, one of the few remaining toll bridges on the Thames. At one time, pedestrians were charged a fee; as a result, poorer people crossed the river by the weir upstream. Walk away from the bridge along the path. A small part of Pangbourne Meadow is controlled by the National Trust, and the area is often quite busy with dog walkers, strollers, children kayaking in the river and boat people on their moored vessels. The meadow narrows at the end, but the path continues through a kissing gate into the next field.

Once beyond the meadow you are unlikely to be disturbed by others for some time, and you are free to watch the ducks and swans feeding from the riverbed. A great variety of plants thrive on the riverbank, and in summer it is lined with white, gold, red and purple wild flowers such as willowherb, goldenrod, bitter-sweet and wild clary. Along all of this stretch, the view to the right is over open fields. On the left, apart from a few spots that are blocked by willows and tall hawthorn bushes, there are sweeping views of the Chilterns, their steep slopes partly wooded, partly bare.

Watch out for the many molehills beside the path, which indicate lots of underground activity. Sadly, you are unlikely to see any of the riverside creatures made famous by Kenneth Grahame in *The Wind in the Willows* (1908) – moles, water rats, badgers and otters. The last three are now rarely spotted, and the mole remains as reclusive as depicted in the book.

As you cross a small concrete bridge, notice a pretty, reed-filled stream coming down from the right to enter the Thames. The walk returns along this stream, giving you the chance to explore it more closely. Continue along the riverside path from field to field, going through kissing gates where necessary. After a while, you will see Hardwick Stud Farm on the opposite bank, a long house with a white upper storey, set back from fields in which horses graze. Shortly beyond this, briefly visible between dense stands of trees, is Hardwick House, a grand, gabled Tudor residence. Elizabeth I and later Charles I once stayed here, the latter playing bowls on the lawn by the river.

It has been suggested that Toad Hall in *The Wind in the Willows* was based on either Hardwick House or Mapledurham House, a little further downstream, since Kenneth Grahame lived in nearby Pangbourne. However, the story is probably based on recollections of childhood days in Cookham Dean, making Harleyford Manor near Marlow (see page 99) a more likely candidate.

Mapledurham Lock

When you see an isolated house on the hill opposite, the riverside section of this walk is near its end. The river begins to turn south, and a glimpse of Mapledurham Church and Mill can be seen between the trees opposite Mapledurham Lock.

The lock at Mapledurham is one of the prettiest on the whole river, particularly in summer when the flower beds are ablaze with colour. In the past, the trim lawn and well-kept gardens have won the local lock keeper a number of awards. A signpost for boaters informs them that they are 78½ miles from London and 33 miles from Oxford.

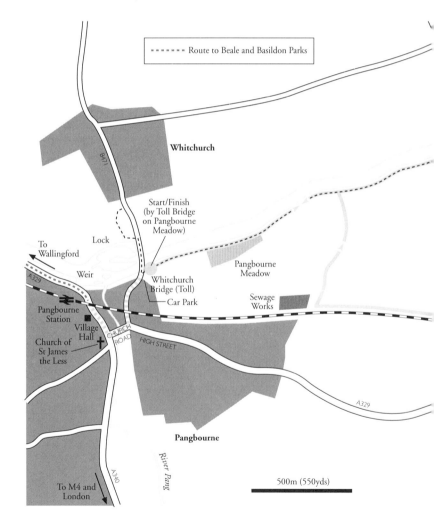

In summer, tea is available and there are sometimes plants for sale. If you need a rest before the return leg of the walk, relax on a bench and watch the boats come and go.

Back by the Railway
Leave the lock by a gate at the far end. To continue the walk, keep to the right across the field to a barred gate, but if you are curious to look at Mapledurham House itself, carry on by the riverside a little. The house has belonged to the Blount family since it was built in 1588. Alexander Pope used to be a visitor here in the early 18th century, and wrote verses for Teresa and Martha Blount, the latter having won his heart. The house is open to the public, but is inaccessible from this bank.

Go back to the barred gate and through the kissing gate beside it, then go straight

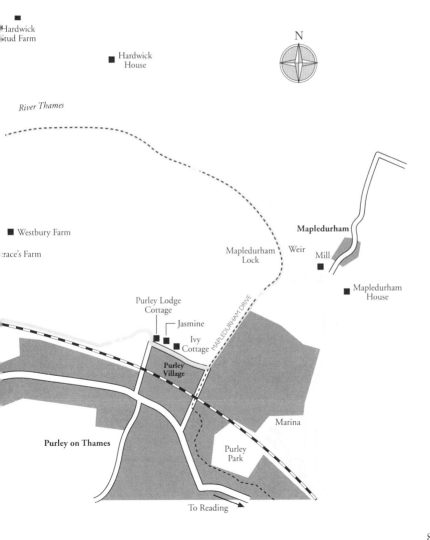

ahead on a gravel drive, which becomes a sealed lane. This is Mapledurham Drive, which leads down to the lock. On the left there is an odd mix of old and new houses, the fringe of Purley's and Reading's urban sprawl, and on the right there are open fields.

At the top of the drive, you leave the Thames Path, which goes straight ahead through suburban streets to rejoin the river at Reading, and turn right into Purley Village. Go up a slight rise and pass some attractive old cottages – Ivy Cottage, Jasmine and Purley Lodge Cottage. Where the road bends sharply to the left, turn right into a public bridleway. This begins as a broad gravel drive, but quickly narrows to a dirt track. It bends to the left behind houses, then climbs gently to the top of a railway cutting.

On the left, the path is overgrown with hawthorn and brambles, but there is a beautiful sweeping view of the valley to the right, which continues for about 1.5 kilometres (1 mile). Soon, you pass some allotments on the right and a bridge over the railway on the left. This is the first of three bridges you will pass. Keep going straight on to the next bridge. You may notice small cylindrical markers at ankle height; these are boundary markers for the railway, dated 1890. Go straight ahead at the second bridge, taking a footpath that dips down so that the railway is now above you, on an embankment. To the right across a field are farm buildings, and the embankment on the left is thick with willowherb and brambles.

At the end of the third field, beside another railway bridge, you come to a stile. Turn right just before it and walk along the left-hand side of the field beside a narrow stream. A tall fence beyond the stream surrounds a sewage works, but the stream itself is a delight. As you follow it down to the Thames, notice the many wild flowers and reeds on its banks, and the lilies and ducks floating on its surface.

The winding path takes you into another field and over a stile before rejoining the Thames. You will find yourself beside the small concrete bridge that you passed early on the walk. From here, simply walk back upstream through Pangbourne Meadow to the bridge, where the walk ends. From here, you might want to hunt out refreshment in Pangbourne, take a walk around the village, or head for Beale or Basildon Park.

Options – Beale Park and Basildon Park

Take the A329 west out of Pangbourne, passing between grand Victorian mansions and the Thames. Within five minutes' drive, you will arrive at Beale Park on the right, and just beyond a railway bridge, Basildon Park on the left. Beale Park is a wildlife centre that is a veritable wonderland for children. It has a miniature train, adventure playground, paddling pools, a crazy golf course and a sandpit, as well as many animals, such as deer, llamas, Shetland ponies, and common farmyard animals. There are also many unusual birds such as flamingoes and snowy owls.

Basildon Park is a grand 18th-century Palladian mansion built of honey-coloured Bath stone, set on a hill and surrounded by woodland. Since 1978, it has been run by the National Trust. The house has interesting plasterwork, paintings and furniture, and the ground floor is now used as a tea room. If you have time, you might like to stroll through the 160 hectares (400 acres) of parkland and woodland. Two marked walks, the Pheasant Park Walk and Woodland Walk, lead over fields and through dense woodland consisting of oak, beech, chestnut, larch and lime. Occasional evening concerts are held on the lawn in front of the house in summer (contact the National Trust for details).

Sonning

Summary: Situated at a natural fording point, Sonning is a strong contender for the label 'prettiest village on the Thames'. Its layout has hardly changed since Saxon times; its buildings are rich with history, and the 18th-century brick bridge and former mill create an idyllic scene. The walk passes along a stretch of uninhabited, lush riverbank, climbs up to the fields and copses of the lower Chilterns, then returns back down to the river.

Location:	57 kilometres (36 miles) west of London.
Start/Finish:	At the northwest corner of Sonning Bridge, on the B478. OS Explorer map 171, GR 755758.
Visitor attractions:	Pretty buildings in Sonning; peaceful stretch of riverside; bluebells in Shiplake Copse (spring); views from Chilterns.
Access:	(*by car*) Sonning lies off the A4 between Maidenhead and Reading. Drive through the village on the B478 and cross the bridge. Park in the small car park about 100 metres (110 yards) beyond the bridge on the left, just before the private car park for the French Horn Hotel. Walk back to the bridge. The walk begins on the left just before the bridge.
	(*by bus*) Take a 127 (Reading Buses) from Reading. Walk down through the village and cross the bridge, then turn immediately right along the Thames Path.
	(*by boat*) Salter Brothers' boats link Sonning with Reading and Henley.
Length:	10 kilometres (6 miles).
Time:	3 hours.
Refreshments:	The Tea Cosy or the Bull Inn in Sonning; the Plowden Arms in Shiplake; the Flowing Spring on the return. For a special treat, try the French Horn Hotel (reservations necessary. Tel: 01189 692204).
Pathway status:	Country paths; pavements; wooded tracks.
Best time to visit:	Spring, to see the bluebells in Shiplake Copse.

Background

Sonning is named after Sunna, a Saxon chieftain, who also ruled over places as far away as Sunningdale. By AD 900 it had its own bishop, and for centuries it remained an important ecclesiastical centre with a grand Bishop's palace, now long gone. Isabella de Valois, married to Richard II when she was only eight, was held at the palace in 1399 for a short time when Henry IV seized power from Richard. Several claim to have seen the ghost of a 'lady youthful and fair' walking near the river, sobbing and sighing. Whether she mourns her lost husband or pines for her homeland is not clear. She was eventually sent back to France.

There are several interesting buildings in the village, which can be explored before or after the walk. St Andrew's Church is a huge Victorian structure. Its size is explained by Sonning's ecclesiastical importance – there has been a church on this site since the 9th or 10th century. Just to the east of St Andrew's is The Bull Inn, overlooking a small courtyard. Built in the 16th century, this is a classic country inn with low beams and tobacco-stained walls, and has long been the focal point of village life.

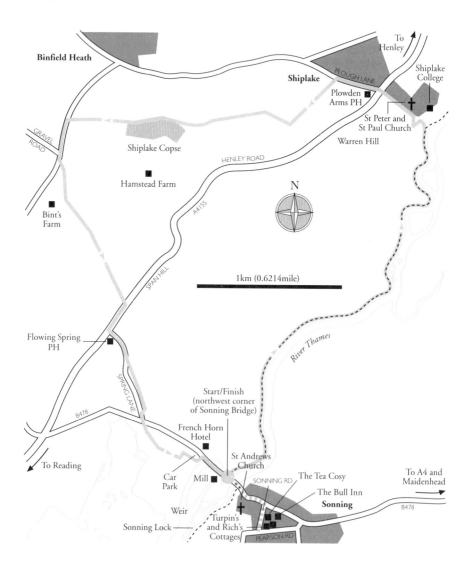

At the junction of Sonning Lane and Pearson Road are two small but significant cottages – Turpin's Cottage and Rich's Cottage. In the mid-18th century,
highway robbers such as Dick Turpin were feared across the land. Legend has it that
after a successful hold-up on the nearby Bath Road, Turpin would come galloping
into Sonning, hotly pursued by the law, and jump into the river. He would then
swim across to Oxfordshire, where Berkshire authorities had no jurisdiction.
Meanwhile, his horse, Black Bess, would find its own way back to a stable beneath
his aunt's house. This was the middle cottage in a row of three, which have now
been knocked into two. Rich's Cottage, as the name suggests, once belonged to
wealthy local landowners.

To see how Sonning maintains its reputation as one of the prettiest villages on
the Thames, take a look at a cluster of cottages on Pearson Road – pale blue shut-
ters, fresh whitewash, hanging baskets and leaning walls all add to the effect. In the
narrow High Street, the solitary Village Store doubles as a tea house (The Tea Cosy).
Sonning Lock, about 200 metres (220 yards) upstream from the bridge, is another
attractive spot.

The Walk

Start at the northwest corner of Sonning road bridge, where a Thames Path sign
points over a footbridge. Sonning Mill is across the road, set among huge plane trees.
This was used from Saxon times right through until 1969, possibly longer than any
other mill on the Thames. It has now been converted into a 'dinner theatre', with
occasional jazz performances.

Cross a wood and concrete bridge over a Thames backwater that flows from
under the mill. From the bridge, you can see the impressive grounds of the French
Horn Hotel to the left, with weeping willows drooping down into the water. Turn
right along the path after the bridge, then follow it round. You will soon get a view
of the road bridge and its arches through the willows. If boats are about, notice that
the central arch leaves little room for error as they pass through. The path now
begins to meander northeast beside the river towards Shiplake.

A Confident River

On this stretch, the river passes confidently through low meadows, gliding around
densely-wooded islands with the Chilterns on its left. The path snakes beside it, passing
through woodland or past open fields. For most of the way, the riverbank is bordered
by trees and bushes. You will probably spot familiar plants – thistles and nettles, alders,
sycamores, and wheat in the fields. Look out for ducks and moorhens near the shore,
and herons standing in the shallows.

After about 3 kilometres (1¾ miles), the path goes over a small footbridge beside
the boatyards of Shiplake College, and at this point the walk turns away from the
river. Do not follow the private path up to the college, but turn sharp left along a
footpath behind the boathouse, and start to climb a hill. After a few strides, turn
sharp right where the path meets a farm track, and follow a footpath up a steep slope

until it comes out by St Peter and St Paul Church. This building has many ancient features, including a 15th-century stained glass window showing a vision of the Crucifixion and the Coronation of the Virgin. It is also where, in 1850, the poet Alfred Lord Tennyson married Emily Sellwood after a 20-year engagement (his in-laws had their doubts about his religious orthodoxy).

Into the Chilterns

Bear to the left of the church and go down Church Lane to the main Henley Road. The is a fast road, so cross it carefully, then go straight ahead into Plough Lane beside the Plowden Arms. Pass the beginning and end of Plowden Lane on the right, then take a left into a sealed road that seems to go nowhere. Where it turns left to a farm-yard, go straight ahead through an iron kissing gate and on up a gentle rise at the side of a field. Note that the fence is electrified. At the end of the field, go over a stile with a concrete step, then turn right, along the side of another field. In the next corner, turn left and go round to the left of a small copse.

About 50 metres (55 yards) beyond the copse, follow a wooden arrow on a telegraph pole that points up to the right. Climb steadily through a field that may become rather overgrown in summer, up towards woodland. At the corner of the field, go through a gap in the trees and continue in the same direction, crossing another path, and then across another field. The path rises to an oak tree, then dips again to enter Shiplake Copse over a stile. Here, you climb steeply for a short distance amongst majestic beech trees, fallen tree trunks and a carpet of bluebells in spring.

Near the top of the rise, cross another stile and follow the fence beside an open field on the right. For a short way, there is dense woodland on the left. Continue to the end of this field and along the side of another, until you come out on a sealed road. You will see a few houses, part of the small village of Binfield Heath. Turn left and walk through the rest of the village. Once Gravel Road has joined from the right, the road bends left then right past the simple village church. On the right-hand bend, turn left, walk down a gravel drive and then straight ahead on a wooded footpath.

Down to the Riverside

Where the path crosses a farm track, go straight ahead and begin the downhill walk towards a line of poplars, passing beneath an oak tree. Ahead, you begin to see a lovely view of rolling hills and meadows, stretching for 20 kilometres (12 miles) or more. The path descends quite steeply with dense woodland on the right, followed by thick shrubs bordering the path. Follow it all the way back down to the main Henley Road. Turn right, cross the road with care, and walk down to the Flowing Spring pub about 100 metres (110 yards) ahead at the junction with Spring Lane. The spring is among a stand of tall trees opposite the pub.

Turn into Spring Lane, which is narrow but can be busy. Just 50 metres (55 yards) along the lane, a small bridge crosses a clear stream. If you pause here, you may be lucky enough to spot a kingfisher darting in and out of the water. After another 50 metres (55 yards), turn left over a stile into a field to escape the traffic.

Follow the path along the right of this field, over stiles, a small bridge and along the right of a second field. At the end of this field, leave by a stile in the right-hand corner. Continue down the last 100 metres (110 yards) of Spring Lane, past the first houses of Sonning Eye, to the main road (B478).

Cross the road and go straight ahead through a gateway on to a dead-end street. Follow this until it turns sharp left (marked with large arrows), then go straight ahead into another backstreet. Just before a sharp left bend, notice an ancient building with worn beams and warped walls on the right. Follow the road round, then after a few more steps turn right on to a footpath. This leads to the back of the car park beside the backwater of the Thames.

Henley

Summary: Henley is perhaps associated with the Thames more than any other town, particularly because of its world-famous annual regatta. This walk follows the regatta course from Henley Bridge, along Henley Reach and past the small village of Remenham. It then swings around a huge bend in the river to Hambleden Lock, which has one of the most impressive weirs on the Thames, and the picturesque Hambleden Mill. From the site of the old Aston Ferry, the walk turns away from the river and goes over the lower slopes of Remenham Hill, offering expansive views across the Thames Valley to the Chilterns. Near the end of the walk, the path also passes through attractive woodland. The River & Rowing Museum (see option) offers an excellent introduction to the town, the Thames and the sport of rowing.

Location:	61 kilometres (38 miles) west of London.
Start & Finish:	Outside the Leander Club, at the northeast corner of Henley Bridge. OS Explorer map 171, GR 765826.
Visitor attractions:	River & Rowing Museum (option); Henley Regatta course; Hambleden Weir and Mill; views of the Chilterns from Remenham Hill.
Access:	(*by car*) Henley lies on the A4130 between Maidenhead and Wallingford. Take the road heading south from the west side of the bridge (by the Angel on the Bridge), and follow it round by the river. Just after the road bends away from the river (by Hobb's Boatyard), turn left into Meadow Road to the Pay & Display car park. If you plan to visit the River & Rowing Museum (see option), drive on through to the museum car park, which is free for 4 hours. From either car park, walk across Mill Meadows to the riverside, turn left and follow along to the bridge. Cross the bridge, cross the road, and the Leander Club is the first building on the left.
	(*by train*) Take a train from Paddington to Twyford, then change for Henley. Turn right out of the station, then right again (Meadow Lane) for the River & Rowing Museum, or go down to the riverside beside Hobb's Boatyard to follow the main walk. Turn left and walk along to Henley Bridge. Cross the bridge and turn first left. The Leander Club is the first building on the left.
	(*by boat*) Salter Brothers' boats link Henley with Reading and Marlow.
Length:	8 kilometres (5 miles).
Time:	2½ hours.
Refreshments:	The Flower Pot in Aston; pubs, restaurants and cafés in Henley,

including the Henley Tea Rooms, southwest of Henley Bridge.

Pathway status: Towpath; country lanes and paths; wooded tracks; pavements.

Best time to visit: Any time except the first week of July when the regatta takes place, since much of the path is inaccessible.

Background

Henley developed as an inland port during medieval times, but it is now a bustling market town with many attractive Tudor and Georgian buildings around the town centre. The most obvious landmark is the Church of St Mary the Virgin, which has overlooked the bridge and the river for almost 800 years. In the passageway to the left of the church entrance is the Chantry House, which dates back to the 15th century, and a row of almshouses.

In nearby New Street is Brakspear's Brewery, the oldest independent brewery in Oxfordshire; and further up this street, walking away from the river, is the Kenton Theatre, which has been open since 1805. Bell Street and Duke Street, both in the town centre, are full of trendy boutiques and antique shops. In Friday Street there are many attractive old buildings as well as Richard Way Books, an excellent source of books about the Thames – new, rare and second-hand.

The Walk

Option – River & Rowing Museum

The River & Rowing Museum, situated by the Thames at the south end of Mill Meadows (see map), has two large galleries dedicated to the River Thames and the sport of rowing, as well as a small gallery about Henley itself. It therefore makes a perfect introduction to the area. Many of the displays are interactive, and touch-screen exhibits enhance the static displays. There are also a few smaller galleries housing temporary exhibitions, a shop and an attractive café.

The Thames gallery is particularly interesting if you have walked, or plan to walk, significant sections of the Thames Path. It begins with examples of paintings and music inspired by the Thames, followed by an intriguing display of ancient implements found in the river, believed to be ritual offerings. There are then displays about more modern aspects of the river, such as the introduction of locks and weirs, and finally a miniature version of the Thames Barrier, illustrating a major achievement of modern technology.

The Regatta Course

The Leander Club, where the walk begins, is the world's most prestigious rowing club and host to the Henley Royal Regatta each July. Walk past it and down to the riverside. At any time of year, you may see rowers practising here, and in summer the area around the bridge is busy with many types of pleasure craft. The 18th-century bridge, which has masks of Father Thames and the Goddess Isis over both sides of the central arch, and the tower of St Mary's Church opposite, form one of the most famous views along the Thames.

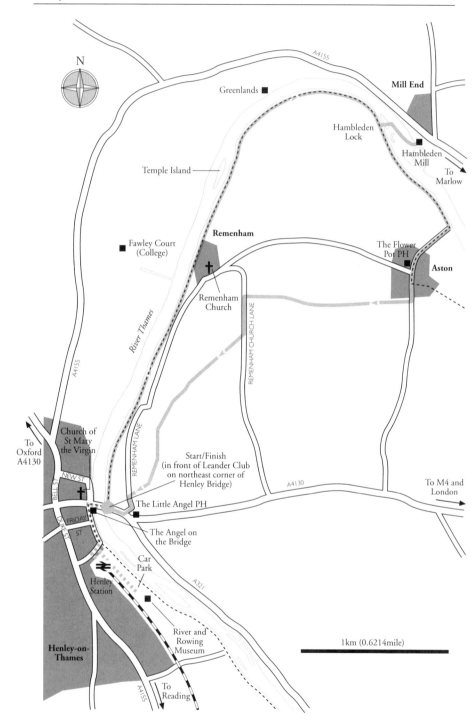

N

Mill End

Greenlands

Hambleden
Lock

Hambleden
Mill

To
Marlow

Temple Island

Remenham

The Flower
Pot PH

Aston

Fawley Court
(College)

Remenham
Church

REMENHAM CHURCH LANE

River Thames

A4155

Church of
St Mary
the Virgin

REMENHAM LANE

To
Oxford
A4130

Start/Finish
(in front of Leander Club
on northeast corner of
Henley Bridge)

A4130

To M4 and
London

NEW ST

The Little Angel PH

BELL ST

FRIDAY ST

DUKE ST

The Angel on
the Bridge

Car
Park

Henley
Station

A321

River and
Rowing
Museum

1km (0.6214mile)

Henley-on-
Thames

A4155

To
Reading

Walk northwards on the ample riverbanks of the historic Henley Reach. This is one of the few places where the Thames ceases to meander, providing a straight course for rowers. The first Oxford and Cambridge boat race was held here in 1829, and from 1839 the Henley Regatta has taken place on this stretch every year (apart from during the two world wars). The regatta gained its 'Royal' tag in 1851, when it came under the patronage of Prince Albert.

The village of Remenham is on the right after about 1.5 kilometres (1 mile), and you can see its church beyond the riverside dwellings. Continue along the path and you soon pass Temple Island, named after the curious building constructed to enhance the view from Fawley Court on the opposite side of the river. It has a domed roof and columns, protecting a classical sculpture within. The island now belongs to the regatta organizers. The regatta course, which is 1 mile 550 yards long (just under 2 kilometres), starts at the north end of this island.

Hambleden Lock and Mill

The path beside Henley Reach is sealed to enable rowing coaches to cycle alongside the crews, so the walking from here up to Hambleden Lock is very easy. Beyond Temple Island, the river begins to veer around an enormous bend to the right, and an area of open meadows comes into view. On the opposite bank you can see the imposing structure of Greenlands, a white, Italianate mansion, with huge cypress trees set in a trim lawn. This was built in 1853 for the famous bookseller W.H. Smith (1825–91), who later became Viscount Hambleden. His heirs eventually donated almost 1,600 hectares (4,000 acres) of the Greenlands Estate to the National Trust, which you will pass through on your way back to Henley. These days, Greenlands is the site of Henley Management College.

The river continues to sweep around from east to southeast, and shortly passes Hambleden Lock. Pass through a gate into the lock area. The walk continues on the same side of the river, but you might like to make a short detour here to look at Hambleden weir and mill. To do this, cross over the lock and follow the walkway over one of the widest and most impressive weirs on the whole river. Mallards can often be seen standing in the shallow water, dipping their heads into the fast flow to feed. The former Hambleden Mill, situated at the end of the walkway, has been converted into private apartments. However, it has retained its attractive weather-boarded appearance and is one of the most photographed structures along the Thames.

Back on the south bank, the path continues beyond the lock on a broad gravel drive. This soon turns away from the river, but you should keep to the riverbank, passing through a gate and into a grassy field. The bank is thick with alders here, and there are wooded islands in the river. At the end of the field, go through a gate, over a small wooden footbridge and into a sealed drive. This used to be the access route to the Aston Ferry, which was situated at this point. Turn right and follow it up into the village of Aston.

Through the Greenlands Estate

At Aston, you are about halfway along the walk, and The Flower Pot pub makes a convenient resting point. It has a large garden with apple trees, while inside, the walls are covered with prints of riverside scenes and cases of stuffed fish caught in various parts of the country.

To continue the walk, go straight up from The Flower Pot along Aston Lane, then turn right along a footpath just after Highway Cottage. The path starts climbing here and continues over a stile, then across a field to a short passageway between bushes. Where it joins a broad track coming up the hill from the right, go straight – there are tall trees on the right and an open field on the left. The path levels out here and enters a peaceful area, part of the Greenlands Estate, with views across to the Chilterns on the other side of the river.

The broad track ends by a gate at Remenham Church Lane. Cross the stile beside the gate and turn left. Walk a short distance up the lane and turn right by a public footpath sign, just before a large, solitary oak tree. The path heads diagonally across a field back towards woodland. In summer this field is full of poppies and other colourful wild flowers. Go straight on into the wood, where there are several large beech trees beside the path. At the end, go over another stile and straight ahead across the corner of a sloping field (the path is not clearly defined here), then re-enter a sheltered path ahead.

The path dips down and emerges via a stile on to a well-cut lawn. Head diagonally across this lawn to another stile, passing in front of an imposing house on the hill. Go over the stile and along a gravel drive to a gateway. The footpath leaves the field to the left of the gate and comes out on a sealed road (Remenham Lane). Turn left and follow the lane around a sharp right bend. It comes out on the busy Henley Road, with The Little Angel pub on the left. Turn right, and within a few steps you are back at the Leander Club beside Henley Bridge.

Plate 16: *Hardwick House, a grand Tudor residence visited by both Charles I and Elizabeth I, stands in splendid isolation on the riverbank (see page 81).*

Plate 17: Sonning Mill, which was in use from Anglo-Saxon times to 1969, is now used as a 'dinner theatre' (see page 87).

Plate 18: *A satirical cartoon about the unhealthy state of the Thames, on display at the River & Rowing Museum in Henley (see page 90).*

Plate 19: *Cookham's Tarry Stone was perhaps the point at which athletes waited before competing in village sports (see page 101).*

Plate 20: Ye Olde Bell Inn claims to be the oldest hostelry in England (see page 99).

Plate 21: Eton College students changing classes (see page 107).

Plate 22: The Round Tower at Windsor Castle. The castle, parts of which date from 1070 when William the Conqueror initiated its construction, is the largest continually-inhabited castle in the world (see page 106).

Hurley and Marlow

Summary: This walk forms a lopsided figure of eight rather than a circle, taking in the village of Hurley and the town of Marlow, two of the oldest settlements along the River Thames. Hurley was the scene of a successful plot to overthrow the king and Marlow is associated with several well-known literary figures. The route crosses the river in spectacular style at Temple Footbridge, and passes the sites of Temple Mills and Bisham Abbey, the England football team's training ground.

Location:	49.5 kilometres (31 miles) west of London
Start and finish:	Monks' Barn, on left at north end of Hurley High Street. OS Explorer map 172, GR 825840. (If arriving by train, join the walk in Marlow.)
Visitor attractions:	Priory remains at Hurley; Temple Footbridge; Bisham Abbey; streets of Marlow.
Access:	(*by car*) Hurley lies off the A4130 between Maidenhead and Henley. Turn into the single street of the village and park at the end, just beyond the Monks Barn and opposite St Mary's Church.
	(*by train*) Take the train from Paddington to Maidenhead, then the branch line to Marlow. From the station, walk up Station Approach to The Marlow Donkey pub (named after the train). Turn left into Station Road and join the walk at Marlow Place, at the junction with St Peter's Road.
	(*by boat*) Salter Brothers' boats link Hurley with Henley and Marlow.
Length:	9 kilometres (5½ miles).
Time:	3 hours.
Refreshments:	The Compleat Angler in Marlow; several pubs and cafés on Marlow High Street; Ye Olde Bell in Hurley.
Pathway status:	Towpath; wooded tracks; pavements; country paths.

Background

A church has existed on the site now occupied by St Mary's since 633, giving a good idea of Hurley's great age. After the Norman conquest, a Benedictine priory was also established here. Though the village has always remained small in size, it has been involved in historic events, and claims to have the oldest tavern in the country.

Marlow's population boomed in the late 20th century, and it is now a bustling town. However, its distinctive suspension bridge and Georgian buildings give it an old-world feel, and the spirit of famous writers who once lived here lingers on.

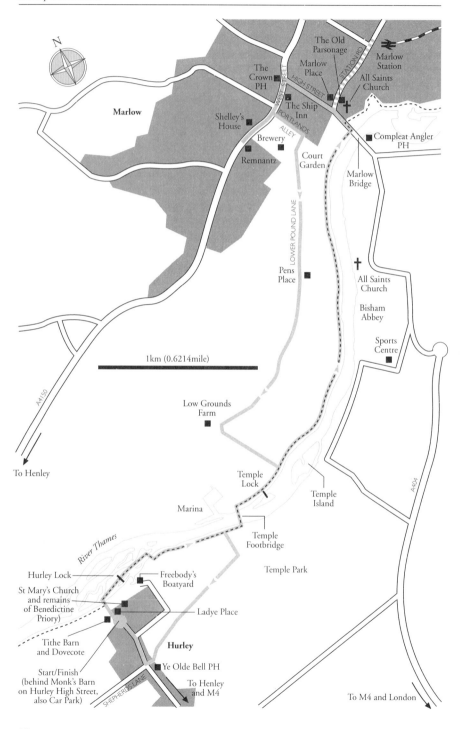

The Walk

Subterranean Plotting by the River

Before setting off along a particularly fine stretch of the river, take a quick look at the remains of the Benedictine priory. Go to the left of St Mary's Church, and look through the arch at the small square. The refectory wall of the priory can still be seen on the left, along with the cloisters straight ahead, now a private residence. Henry VIII dissolved the priory in 1536, and the land was passed on to the Lovelace family who built a Tudor manor called Ladye Place. This stands to the left of the church, though the current building only dates back a hundred years or so.

It was in a vault beneath Ladye Place that members of the Lovelace family, along with other nobles, plotted the overthrow of the Catholic King James II in 1688. A letter was taken down the Thames and delivered to William of Orange in Holland. After the 'Glorious Revolution', he then came to power with Mary as a Protestant monarch. To the left of Ladye Place are two impressive buildings – a former tithe barn and a dovecote. They were built in the 14th century, and a painstaking restoration returned them to their original beauty in the late 20th century.

Follow the footpath between the tithe barn and the high wall of Ladye Place. This leads to a footbridge on to an island, where the lock and weir are located. Turn right and walk the length of the island, passing the lock. Just beyond it on the right is a large boatyard (Freebody's), where boats are made to order and restored using traditional techniques. At the end of the island, cross back to the south bank over another footbridge, then follow the riverside path downstream to Temple Footbridge.

A New Bridge for Walkers

Temple Footbridge was built in 1989, and is perhaps the most significant addition to the entire Thames Path, making it possible to cross from the Berkshire to Buckinghamshire bank for the first time since the ferry service stopped in 1953. (Other new footbridges were opened at Shifford and Bourne End.) At 80 metres (88 yards), this is the longest hardwood bridge in Britain. As you cross it, pause to look downstream at the view of Temple Lock, and back upstream, where a number of cruisers are usually moored beside the Harleyford Marina. Harleyford Manor is obscured by trees, but is possibly the model for Toad Hall in *The Wind in the Willows* (1908), since its author, Kenneth Grahame, spent his childhood at nearby Cookham Dean.

Of Temples, Abbeys and Churches

Beyond the bridge, follow the path past Temple Lock, which is surrounded by bright flowers and also offers tea and cakes in summer. Walk on downstream as the river swings gradually round from west to north. Temple Island, opposite, was named after the Knights Templar who once lived at Bisham Abbey, just downstream. In the late 18th century the island was the site of Temple Mills, run by Sir Thomas Williams. He was known as the 'Copper King' and was the dominant force in the British copper industry, which in those days produced more than half the world's output. What you now see are modern developments, and no sign of the mills remains today.

Continue on past open fields on the left, and soon you will pass a small boathouse on the far bank belonging to Bisham Abbey. Little can be seen of the former abbey buildings from the north bank of the river, but keep an eye out for famous faces in the grounds, for the property now belongs to the National Sports Council and is occasionally used as a training ground by the England football team.

Bisham Abbey has played a vital role in English history. The site was granted to the Knights Templar in the 12th century; then in 1536, after the dissolution of the monasteries, Henry VIII gave it to Anne of Cleves. She passed it on to Sir Philip Hoby (pronounced 'Hobby') who sheltered the Princess Elizabeth, exiled from court during the reign of her half-sister Mary (1553–58).

Sir Philip's wife, also named Elizabeth, became known as 'the old lady of splendid sorrows' after a lifetime of organizing funerals for two husbands and four children. Legend has it that she killed one of her children, either by beating him or locking him in a cupboard, in anger at his inability to write. Some claim to have seen her ghost walking the grounds of the abbey, wringing her hands in remorse. There may be some truth in the legend, as blotted copybooks were discovered beneath floorboards during alterations to the building in 1840.

Beyond the abbey grounds, the solid Norman tower of All Saints Church stands near the riverbank. After this you pass a number of spacious garden lawns, a sign that you are nearing Marlow. Soon you leave open fields behind to enter Higginson Park. Walk up to the suspension bridge and on up to the road. (If you would rather avoid Marlow, cut across Higginson Park. A footpath leads left through the trees to Lower Pound Lane, and you can return to Hurley from there.)

Around Marlow

Marlow suspension bridge was built by Tierney Clarke in 1832. It is the town's best-known landmark and is one of the most attractive bridges over the Thames. On the far bank beyond the bridge is the famous Compleat Angler Hotel, named after Izaak Walton's 17th-century treatise on angling. The name dates from the late 19th century, when its owner chose it to appeal to the rich socialites who took to the river each summer. To the left of the bridge is All Saints Church, which dominates the Marlow skyline with its tall, slender spire. The pretty lock and weir are situated downstream.

Walk away from the bridge to explore the town. Turn right into Station Road to see The Old Parsonage and Marlow Place, two of the town's oldest buildings, near each other on the corner of St Peter's Street. (**Walkers arriving by train** join here.) Parts of The Old Parsonage date from the 14th century and its windows peek out from creeper-covered walls. Marlow Place is grander, and was a royal residence during the days of George II and III. It is now a listed building occupied by a private company.

Go back to the High Street, which is predominantly Georgian, and turn right. At the top end is The Crown pub, which was once the Town Hall and an important coaching inn. Jerome K. Jerome (1859–1927) stayed there in 1889; in *Three Men in a Boat*, he describes a procession to the river after a shopping trip in which the characters were followed by the hotel boy, the greengrocer's boy, the baker's boy, the confectioner's boy, the cheesemonger's boy and the fruiterer's boy – a scene you are unlikely to see today.

Turn left at the top of the High Street, into West Street, which also has some significant buildings. The Ship Inn, on the left, is a quaint pub with original 16th-century timbers. Continue to Remnantz, also on the left and built in 1720. This was the original site of the Royal Military College before it was moved to Sandhurst. Albion House, on the right just before the Sir William Borlase School, was home to Percy and Mary Shelley in 1817–19, while he wrote *The Revolt of Islam* and she wrote *Frankenstein*.

Retrace your steps and go right down Portlands Alley, just before the junction with Oxford Road. At the end of the alley, turn right into Pound Lane.

A Countryside Stroll Back to Hurley

Turn first left from Pound Lane into Lower Pound Lane and follow it right to the end. This passes paths leading left to the riverside, which you could take if you prefer, then crosses a pretty stream and goes past Pens Place. At the end, cross a stile beside a barred gate and walk along the left side of a long field. Here you are walking parallel to the river, which is just away to your left. At the end of the field, turn left on to a broad gravel track that leads down to the river. Turn right along the river, back past Temple Lock and over Temple Footbridge again.

Follow the path upstream under giant chestnuts for a short way, then turn left into the woods on a signposted footpath. At the end, turn right on to a gravel drive and continue straight on. Where the road bends to the right, go straight ahead on a footpath that leads to Hurley High Street, opposite Shepherds Lane. On the left here is Ye Olde Bell, which is claimed to be the country's oldest hostelry. It dates back to 1135 and was originally a hospice for visitors to the Benedictine priory; the Sanctus Bell, depicted on the sign over the entrance, was rung to signal the arrival of important visitors. A secret underground passage (now blocked up) links the inn with the priory grounds near the riverside. With its low-beamed interior and trim garden, this makes an ideal spot to take a rest.

Turn right from the footpath or pub and stroll down Hurley High Street, past the Manor House and quaint post office at the end of the row of Church Cottages. You will soon find yourself back at the Monks' Barn and St Mary's Church.

Cookham and Cliveden Reach

Summary: This walk takes you through the village of Cookham, where you can take a look at the paintings of Sir Stanley Spencer and ponder the origins of the Tarry Stone. From here the route follows Cliveden Reach, one of the prettiest stretches of the Thames, where dense woods cover a steep chalk bank. After passing Boulter's Lock, scene of much gaiety in Edwardian times, you return via the Green Way, passing the open spaces of Widbrook Common and good views of Cliveden House.

Location:	45 kilometres (28 miles) west of London.
Start and finish:	The war memorial at the west end of Cookham High Street. OS Explorer map 172, GR 895854.
Visitor attractions:	Stanley Spencer Gallery; Tarry Stone; Cliveden Reach; Boulter's Lock; Ray Mill Island; Widbrook Common; Cliveden House (option).
Access:	(*by car*) Cookham lies north of Maidenhead on the A4094. Turn left into the High Street and continue on to Cookham Moor, where you can park on the right. Walk back to the war memorial on the right at the end of the High Street.
	(*by train*) Take the train from Paddington to Maidenhead and change for Cookham. Turn right down Station Hill. Go straight across a mini-roundabout and along The Pound, passing The Old Swan Uppers and Spencer's pubs, to Cookham Moor. Go straight ahead across the moor to the war memorial on the right at the end of the High Street.
	(*by boat*) Salter Brothers' boats link Boulter's Lock with Windsor and Marlow.
Length:	9 kilometres (5½ miles).
Time:	3 hours.
Refreshments:	Tea shop (in summer) and Boulter's Inn on Ray Mill Island; several pubs and restaurants in Cookham.
Pathway status:	Towpath; wooded tracks; pavements; country paths.
Best time to visit:	The Hanging Woods of Cliveden are at their most impressive in autumn. See Opening Times for the Stanley Spencer Gallery and Cliveden House.

Background

Cookham is famous for a bizarre lump of rock (the Tarry Stone), an eccentric and visionary painter (Sir Stanley Spencer), its parish church, and the villagers' struggles to keep their rights to the moors and commons that lie around. Local residents also held the post of Queen's Swan Marker during much of the 20th century, giving Cookham a close connection with the annual swan-upping ceremony that takes place on the Thames in the third week of July. The ritual involves swan markers, dressed in their finery, rowing up the river in flag-bearing skiffs from Sunbury to Abingdon, ringing all newborn cygnets.

The Walk

A Visionary Painter and a Stone from Nowhere

From the war memorial, walk east along Cookham High Street, passing old pubs, Indian, Italian and Chinese restaurants, and upmarket boutiques in Cookham Arcade. Look for a blue plaque on the wall of Fernlea, on the right just before the Two Roses Restaurant, marking the birthplace of Sir Stanley Spencer.

On the right at the end of the High Street is a former Methodist chapel, now the Stanley Spencer Gallery (small admission charge, see Opening Times). A visit is highly recommended. Sir Stanley Spencer (1891–1959) used local settings in his evocative religious paintings such as *Christ Preaching at Cookham Regatta* and *The Last Supper*, both of which are in the gallery. Several of Spencer's other works are on display in the Tate British art gallery.

A classic English eccentric, Spencer wandered around the village pushing his equipment along in a battered pram (now on show in the gallery) and hung up a 'do not disturb' sign once he had started work. His style is wholly individual and defies easy classification. Most of his subjects are rendered through a distorted perspective, yet in amazing detail. Some paintings feature aspects of local culture, such as the yearly swan-upping ceremony, and it is possible to spot the local church, moor and High Street in some of the backgrounds. Though he was less than five feet tall, his canvases were sometimes enormous: so much so that he had to place his chair on a table to work on them. He was knighted in his last year of life.

To look at the Tarry Stone and the local church, you take a brief detour from the main route and go left at the end of the High Street. The Tarry Stone is set in the pavement, across the road on the next corner. It is a sarsen, a form of sandstone. Its origin is unknown, but it has certainly been here for hundreds of years and is mentioned in many historical documents. A plaque on it claims that before 1507, it was used in connection with village sports, and may have been the spot where competitors waited, or tarried.

Beyond the Tarry Stone, you can find Holy Trinity Church down the small lane to the left. It dates back to Norman times and its interior is packed with statues of local heroes. One of these is Stephen Darby, who unearthed much of Cookham's Roman and Saxon past and published the first history of Cookham in 1831. A reproduction of Spencer's *Last Supper* hangs on the far wall, and his grave is on the right as you leave the church. The churchyard was also the inspiration for Spencer's *Resurrection in Cookham Churchyard*, in which the graves spring open and locals clamber out yawning and chatting with each other.

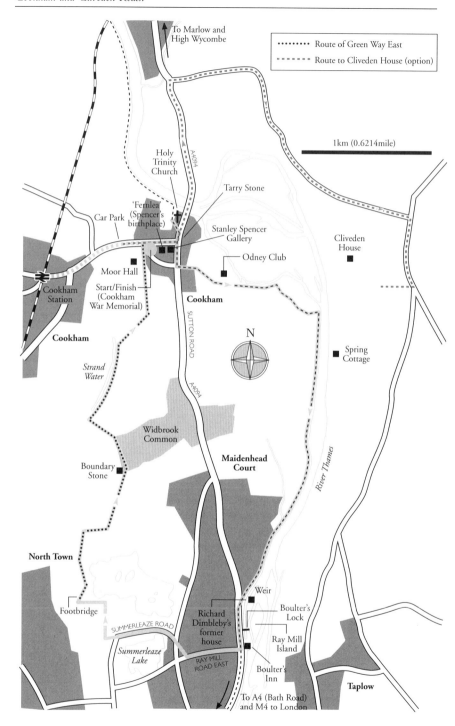

To Marlow and
High Wycombe

········· Route of Green Way East

- - - - - Route to Cliveden House (option)

1km (0.6214mile)

Holy
Trinity
Church

A4094

Tarry Stone

Stanley Spencer
Gallery

'Fernlea'
(Spencer's
birthplace)

Car Park

Odney Club

Cliveden
House

Moor Hall

Start/Finish
(Cookham
War Memorial)

Cookham

N

SUTTON ROAD

Cookham

Cookham
Station

Spring
Cottage

*Strand
Water*

A4094

Widbrook
Common

**Maidenhead
Court**

River Thames

Boundary
Stone

North Town

Footbridge

Weir

Boulter's
Lock

SUMMERLEAZE ROAD

Richard
Dimbleby's
former
house

Ray Mill
Island

*Summerleaze
Lake*

RAY MILL
ROAD EAST

Boulter's
Inn

Taplow

To A4 (Bath Road)
and M4 to London

Jerome's Delight

Return to the Spencer Gallery on the corner of the High Street. From here, walk south on Sutton Road (A4094) for about 100 metres (110 yards). Take the turning for Mill Lane on the left and walk on past a cricket pitch, part of the grounds of the Odney Club. Just before the end of the lane, look for a Thames Path signpost on the right. Follow the narrow pathway as it bends to the left, crosses a driveway, then plunges through dense woods on the way to the river.

At the riverside is a broken concrete jetty. This marks the former landing stage of My Lady Ferry, which stopped running in 1956 and was the last ferry to be operated by the Thames Conservancy. The cottage opposite is Seven Gable Cottage, part of the Cliveden Estate. A little further downstream is Spring Cottage, where John Profumo, Secretary of State for War in the early 1960s, met Christine Keeler, with whom he then began an affair. It transpired that Ms Keeler was also involved with a Russian diplomat, and Profumo was forced to resign in 1963 – the culmination of what was known as the Profumo Affair. This was the last of a chain of scandalous events connected with Cliveden House (see page 107), which sits on a plateau above the woods.

Turn right to wander along the beautiful banks of Cliveden Reach, of which Jerome K. Jerome (1859–1927) wrote, 'In its unbroken loveliness this is, perhaps, the sweetest stretch of all the river.' (*Three Men in a Boat*, 1889). Little has changed since Jerome's day and in summer the path is lined with wild flowers and shrubs – buttercups, thistles, dog roses, elderberry bushes and many others. In autumn, the trees on the opposite bank form a patchwork of green, gold, red and brown as the leaves turn colour. These are the Hanging Woods of Cliveden, so called because of the way the trees cling to the chalk cliffs. If you look back, you may catch glimpses of Cliveden House, but you will get better views of it on the return leg.

A High Society Hang-out

As you walk on, the hills opposite gradually get lower, then the first houses of Maidenhead begin to appear on the right, set well back from the river. Soon, the river widens out, and the rushing sound of the weir signals that you are approaching Boulter's Lock. Just beyond the weir, look for a wooden cottage on the opposite bank, a former home of Richard Dimbleby (1913–65). Dimbleby became one of the first familiar faces of English television in the 1950s and 60s as a pioneer news observer, war correspondent and commentator on royal occasions. A few steps further on, the road (A4094) joins the path on the right and runs alongside it down to Boulter's Lock.

Early in the 20th century, the lock became a famous Ascot Sunday hang-out for members of high society, and the throng of Edwardian river-goers is depicted in the painting *Boulter's Lock – Sunday Afternoon* by E.J. Gregory (1851–1909). Gregory was President of the Institute of Painters in Watercolour, and spent his last years in nearby Marlow. Boulter's is still often busy in summer. Ray Mill Island, behind the lock, has well laid-out gardens, a tea shop open in summer, a small collection of birds and animals and a good view of the water thundering over the weir. Boulter's Inn, beside the lock, has a terrace with fine views down the river.

From the lock, turn right into Ray Mill Road East, a shady suburban street of Maidenhead. Just after The Pagoda (a street, not a building) on the right, turn right down a dark, sheltered passage. After about 200 metres (220 yards) this leads into Sheephouse Road. Cross over and go along Summerleaze Road, noticing an attractive lake on the left. Where the road turns sharp left and becomes Blackamoor Lane, turn right towards the entrance of a gravel pit. Turn left before the gateway and follow a wide gravel path around the perimeter of a high fence.

Along the Green Way

The path turns right and later left beside some rusting machinery. From here, follow it over a footbridge, then take a track to the right. This crosses another drive leading to the gravel pit and continues northwards across a field, bringing you to the north-west corner of the gravel pit site. Follow a broad path to the right, until you reach a barred metal gate. Take a narrow path across the field to the left. If you look behind as you walk, you will see the spire of a church rising exactly in line with the path.

At the end of the field, beside a kissing gate, look carefully beneath the bushes to the left for a small carved stone. This is a Maidenhead boundary stone, visited during the 'Beating the Bounds' ceremony, an ancient tradition in which the local mayor and councillors walk the town's limits to check that the stones are still in place. Go through the gate and walk down a slope to a footbridge crossing White Brook. In summer, look out for damselflies here, particularly the banded agrion, which has a vivid blue or green colour.

The bridge leads to Widbrook Common, and from here on there are good views of the stately Cliveden House across to the right, perched high on the hill. The common itself has been a site of dispute over the years. In medieval times, feudal land-lords often set aside patches of infertile land for local people, so that they could graze their cattle and collect firewood. However, down the centuries, many local landowners tried to restrict their public use. As long ago as 1306, locals conflicted with the Abbot of Cirencester over grazing rights, and in protest packed the commons with animals and left them there until they ate the grass bare. So as you stroll freely across Widbrook Common, you have these pugnacious battlers to thank.

Walk along the left of the common, then turn left through another kissing gate and across a field towards a line of trees. There, branch right, ignoring another path that crosses a stream. Walk along with Strand Water, an attractive stream, on your left and open fields on your right. Cross another path, and keep going along the path signposted Green Way East. The Green Way actually goes all the way from Cookham to Bray, passing through Maidenhead.

Soon, the path bends slightly to the left and here you are approaching the end of the walk. Take a last look at the wide-open spaces before a hedge cuts off the view to the right, then pass into a narrow alley between the buildings of Cookham. The large building to your left is Moor Hall, one of Cookham's most palatial residences. In the past it was occupied by a succession of dignitaries, but these days it is home to the Institute of Market Research.

When you emerge from the path, turn right to return to the war memorial. Notice a beautiful old house on the right called Moor End, with warped beams in its wall. Across the road is the Crown pub, where you can enjoy the view across the common with a glass of ale.

Option – Cliveden House

While in the area, you might like to take a closer look at Cliveden House. To get there, turn left out of the car park, left again at the end of Cookham High Street, and go over Cookham Bridge. Take the first right towards Hedsor, then branch right again along Hedsor Hill and Bourne End Road. At the next junction, turn right for the entrance to Cliveden.

This huge stately home dates back to the 17th century and has long been associated with scandals among the upper classes. Its first owner was George Villiers, the Duke of Buckingham, who in 1688 killed Lord Shrewsbury on the terrace in a duel over Lady Shrewsbury. Instead of avoiding the brutal scene, Lady Shrewsbury dressed up as a page and cheered on her lover. The current building was erected in 1851 and was designed by Sir Charles Barry, who also designed the Houses of Parliament. In 1893 it was bought by William Waldorf Astor, an American tycoon who owned most of New York. In 1906 he gave it as a wedding present to his son and daughter-in-law, Lady Nancy Astor, who went on to become Britain's first woman MP. In the 1930s she hosted weekend parties for the rich and famous, who became known as the 'Cliveden Set'.

The house is now an exclusive hotel, though a few of its rooms are open to public view. The main attractions for walkers are the formal and informal gardens (maintained by the National Trust), and the possibly unrivalled views of the Thames. The gardens include formal parterres, a water garden, dramatic statues and impressive topiary. On summer evenings, there are occasional productions of Shakespeare and music concerts in the garden.

Windsor
and Eton

Summary: This ramble provides perspectives on two cornerstones of English culture – Windsor Castle, with its soaring battlements, and Eton College, cradle of the English aristocracy. It can easily be combined with an exploration of the castle and/or college grounds. Starting beneath the imposing walls of the castle, it follows the Thames in a long loop around the edge of Home Park, then crosses the river and returns via a golf course into the grounds of Eton College. (A shorter version of the walk heads back from here along Eton High Street.) Finally, it passes through riverside meadows with magnificent views of the castle.

Location:	32 kilometres (20 miles) west of London.
Start & Finish:	In front of Windsor & Eton Riverside Station. OS Explorer map 160, GR 968773.
Visitor attractions:	Windsor Castle; Eton College; Home Park; the Brocas.
Access:	(*by car*) Windsor lies just south of the M4 motorway (junction 6). Make your way to Riverside Station and go east along the B470 for about 100 metres (110 yards), then park in a Pay & Display car park to the left or right. Walk back to Riverside Station.
	(*by train*) Take a direct train from Waterloo to Windsor & Eton Riverside Station, or go from Paddington to Slough, then change for Windsor & Eton Central. From Central station, walk out to face the castle, turn left and follow the road round to the right, then left. At the traffic light turn right and cross over to Riverside Station.
	(*by boat*) Salter Brothers' boats link Windsor with towns between Marlow and Staines.
Length:	8 kilometres (5 miles); short version 5.5 kilometres (3½ miles).
Time:	2–2½ hours.
Refreshments:	There are countless pubs and restaurants along Eton High Street (including the ancient Cockpit Restaurant) and clustered around the castle in Windsor.
Pathway status:	Towpath; country paths; pavements.

Background

The name 'Windsor' is an abbreviation of 'winding shore', which aptly describes the topography of the Thames at this point. It was the huge loop in the river, combined with the prominent chalk outcrop on which the castle now stands, that made it an ideal location for a fortress. William the Conqueror instigated its construction in around 1070, seeing it as 'a place appearing proper and convenient for a royal retirement on account of the river and its nearness to the forest for hunting, and many other royal conveniences'. Since then almost every succeeding monarch has added to it or improved it in some way, most notably Henry II and Edward III; and it is now the world's largest continually-inhabited castle. It covers 5 hectares (13 acres) of grounds, while the neighbouring Windsor Great Park sprawls over 1,940 hectares (4,800 acres).

Though the castle is the town's main attraction, the Guildhall on the High Street, completed by Christopher Wren in 1687, is also worth a look. The town council insisted on the addition of inner pillars; Wren obliged, but as a private joke positioned them so that they offer no support to the upper floor. The quaint Market Cross House, next to the Guildhall, leans at such an angle that it seems in constant danger of falling down.

Eton College was built by Henry VI in 1440 to educate 70 'poor and worthy scholars'. Since then many of England's Prime Ministers (such as Walpole and Macmillan) and famous writers (like Shelley, Huxley and Orwell) have been educated there, and typical pupils these days are from rich rather than poor backgrounds.

The Walk

Through Home Park
Standing in front of Riverside Station, with the castle high up on your left, turn right and walk to the river. Turn right again and pass the Donkey House pub. A long, narrow island called The Cobblers sits in the middle of the river. The channel flowing round it to the left leads over a weir, and the right channel leads to Romney Lock, just downstream. Go through a gateway on to a fenced path beside the river, then follow a sealed road through a boatyard. To visit Romney Lock, go left at the boatyard through a gate and over a bridge. It is possible to walk the length of the island behind the lock, a good site for birds such as herons, grebes and wagtails.

Carry on downstream through a kissing gate and under the arches of Black Potts railway bridge, a bridge that played a significant part in railway history. Although only a small town, Windsor has two railway stations, a result of intense competition for royal patronage in the Victorian era. As soon as they got permission, a race began between the Great Western and South Western railway companies to be the first to complete a rail line to Windsor.

The South Western had almost finished, and had announced its opening in August 1849, when a girder snapped during the construction of Black Potts bridge. This delayed the completion by four months. Meanwhile, the Great Western company had men working night and day to make the difficult link between Slough and Windsor, which involved the construction of hundreds of arches (to be seen later on the walk) across a flood plain. Isambard Brunel, the Great Western's heroic engineer, rode in glory on the first train to Windsor in October 1849.

Beyond the railway bridge, sycamores and chestnuts line the riverbank and Home Park spreads out to the south, surmounted by the majestic north façade of the castle. This is just a tiny corner of Windsor Great Park. Horse and flower shows are held here in summer, when the area can be busy. Although much of the park is restricted to Crown use, it has many beautiful public areas, such as the Long Walk which heads south from the castle. Pass some houseboats moored on the opposite bank then turn away from the park over Victoria Bridge, which has colourful crests of arms on its piers.

On the Playing Fields of Eton

Keep to the left while crossing the bridge, then after about 50 metres (55 yards) turn sharp left beside a Public Footpath sign. Descend some uneven steps, which may be slippery if wet, into the grounds of Datchet Golf Club. Follow a broad gravel drive to the left. When it ends, continue along the tree line to the left of the golf course, keeping an eye out for wayward golf balls. At the end, keep to the left beside a fence with a flood relief channel behind it. This area is rich in wild flowers, including huge teasel plants in summer. You might also hear the call of parakeets, which have taken up unlikely residence in the area.

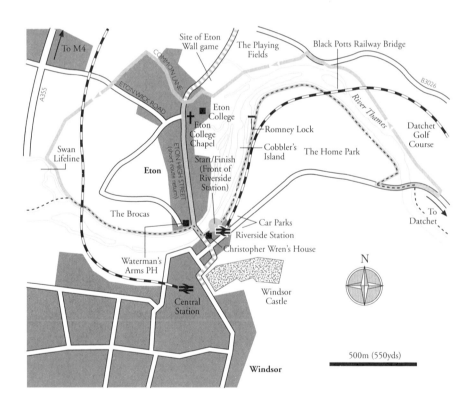

Go under Black Potts railway bridge again, this time under the arches on the north bank, then walk diagonally left across the flood relief scheme. Cross a stile, a drive and another stile and follow the path across the field to yet another stile, which leads out by a boatyard at the river's edge. Follow the driveway beyond the boatyard and come out on to the road (B3026). Turn left and follow the road for about 100 metres (110 yards), then turn left on a gravel path that leads into the grounds of Eton College and over a small, clear stream.

The gravel path follows parallel to the river, and huge trees grace the trim lawn. A cricket pitch and nets lie behind the trees to the right. Pass over a small bridge and on the right, across another manicured lawn, stands a wall with curious white lines painted on it. This is the wall used in the enigmatic Wall Game, a peculiar Etonian invention that seems to combine the skills of football, rugby and mud-wrestling. Directly ahead are the college buildings, some of which are open to the public (see page 153 for tour times). Bear right in front of these, then left through a crumbling archway. Follow the path round, noticing how recent re-building has managed to blend with the original style. As you emerge from the college buildings on to Eton High Street, to the left you can see College Chapel, which looks more like a cathedral with its grandiose pinnacles.

At the High Street, you can shorten the walk by turning left and strolling past the pubs, restaurants and shops that sell rowing and cricket gear, antiques and books, back to the bridge into Windsor. To complete the full walk, cross the road and continue down the dead-end street (Common Lane) opposite, veering right at a fork. During term time, you are likely to see Eton pupils in bow ties and tails in this area, hurrying between classes or milling about the library.

Artists' Inspiration

Go to the end of Common Lane, then past a gate into open country (a sign says 'Private' but it is a public right of way). Keep to the left and follow the path past the back yards of houses. To the right is a long line of arches, part of the successful Brunel railway project mentioned earlier. The path keeps to the left and enters another field. This leads out to the Eton Wick Road (B3026). Cross with care. Walk diagonally right to a sealed path that skirts allotments beside the railway arches. Turn right at the arches and pass under them, following a Public Bridleway sign.

Follow the path diagonally left across a field towards woodland, then go through a gap in the trees and on to a wide drive in front of Swan Lifeline, on Cuckoo Weir Island. Swan Lifeline is a voluntary organization set up to treat injured mute swans. At one time, the use of lead weights by anglers caused the swan population to drop dramatically; it has recovered well, but swans still face a number of threats, such as a drastic reduction in feeding and nesting sites.

Turn left and follow the drive to the end of the high fence, then turn right on to a public footpath. Follow the path along the right edge of a field. This comes to the riverside just a few yards upstream from a graceful viaduct that spans the river in one sweep, taking Brunel's railway into Windsor.

Walk downstream under the viaduct and on to the open expanse of The Brocas, where the path follows the gentle curve of the river back towards Windsor. There are often boats moored along here, taking advantage of the view of the castle across the river (see cover picture). This view has inspired artists down the centuries and is particularly fine on a sunny evening, with the light coming from the west. There are usually swans along this stretch, hoping for titbits from people on the banks.

Head for a gap between the houses at the end of the meadow, which leads through to the Waterman's Arms (*c.*1542), one of Eton's oldest pubs. Walk up to the right of the pub to rejoin Eton High Street. From here, turn left for a further exploration of Eton, or right for the bridge over to Windsor and the start of the walk. Once over the bridge, go left down the steps, passing Christopher Wren's House and Salter's Boats, then turn first right to go back to Riverside Station.

Runnymede

Summary: This walk is quite short and packed with interest. On the way you pass monuments to three historic events – the signing of the Magna Carta, the assassination of J.F. Kennedy and the loss of over 20,000 airmen in World War II. The trail goes up and down a hill with panoramic views, through ancient meadows and beside a pond teeming with life. It finishes by meandering upstream along a lush section of the Thames. An additional option is a visit to Savill Garden, beautifully landscaped and of interest all year round.

Location:	35 kilometres (22 miles) west of London.
Start/Finish:	Pay & Display car park at Runnymede Recreation Ground. OS Explorer map 160, GR 007724.
Visitor attractions:	Magna Carta, J.F. Kennedy and RAF memorials; panoramic views from Cooper's Hill; Langham Ponds and pretty riverside; Savill Garden (option).
Access:	(*by car*) Runnymede is just west of Staines, on the M25 and A30. Drive about 1 kilometre (½ mile) along the A308 heading for Windsor, and turn right into the Pay & Display car park at the recreation ground.
	(*by train*) Take a train from Waterloo to Egham. Turn right out of the station and right again at the junction with the B3407, then left into Homer Road. At the end of Homer Road, cross with care into the meadows. Follow the path that veers slightly right to a stile opposite Runnymede CDC, and join the walk near the end.
	(*by boat*) Salter Brothers' and French Brothers' boats link Runnymede with Windsor and Hampton Court.
Length:	6.5 kilometres (4 miles).
Time:	2 hours.
Refreshments:	Tea shop at Runnymede Recreation Ground; Magna Carta Tea Rooms at north gate to Runnymede.
Pathway status:	Country paths; wooded tracks; sealed roads; towpath.

Background

If all riverside meadows had been left in their natural state, the one at Runnymede would not be particularly unusual. However, most of them have been built on, especially in urban areas such as this, making it something special. Since 1931, it has been administered by the National Trust, and has long been popular with picnickers and boaters. Gateposts and lodges designed by E.L. Lutyens (1869–1944) mark each end of the area.

Since the construction of three memorials in the 1950s and 60s, the meadows at

Runnymede have acquired enormous significance. The first to be erected was the Commonwealth Air Forces Memorial, opened by Queen Elizabeth II in 1953, to commemorate the thousands of airmen who died in World War II. Next, in 1957, came the American Bar Association Memorial to acknowledge the importance of the Magna Carta as the 'symbol of freedom under law'. Finally, the J.F. Kennedy Memorial was given as a gift to the United States by the Queen and her government in 1965, along with the 0.4 hectare (1 acre) of land on which it stands.

The Walk

The Birthplace of Democracy

Begin by walking to the riverside, then turn left and walk upstream around two big bends by the recreation ground. The path takes you very close to the road at one point, but you will soon leave the traffic behind. Dense bushes obscure the river for the most part, though you may catch a glimpse of the thickly-wooded Magna Carta Island, where the historic document is thought to have been signed. When you see a small, domed structure on the lower slopes of the hill to your left, cross the road (A308) with care. Walk across the meadow, which is usually speckled with wild flowers, to reach the American Bar Association Memorial.

Go straight ahead into the small glade surrounded by oak trees. In the centre stands a small, Greek-style temple supported by slender columns, sheltering a stone of granite. This is inscribed with the words 'To Commemorate Magna Carta – Symbol of Freedom under Law'. At the entrance to the area, signboards explain the circumstances surrounding the event and the dedication of the monument.

The date 15 June 1215 is etched into the memory of every English schoolchild. This was when the unpopular King John was forced to sign a charter limiting his far-reaching powers, and proposing the equality of all men before the law. The barons who made this possible had tired of the king's inept rule, and insisted on a programme of reform that took the form of a charter of liberties. Having seized control of London, they came here from Staines, while John came from his strong-hold at Windsor Castle; and the Magna Carta was signed.

A copy of this famous document is posted at the memorial site. The key words lie in clause 39, which states that 'No free man shall be taken, imprisoned, outlawed, banished or in any way destroyed, nor will we proceed against or prosecute him, except by lawful judgement of his equals and by the law of the land.' However, many other parts of the charter throw light on the state of England in the 13th century. These include a promise to remove all fish weirs from the Thames, as they were a hindrance to transport and trade; to standardize weights and measures; to abolish all evil customs connected with forests (whatever they might have been); and to banish all foreign knights who came to harm the kingdom.

American Soil in England

After contemplating the charter, leave the memorial and turn left. Walk along by a hedge for 50 metres (55 yards), then go through a kissing gate. This is the entrance to the Kennedy Memorial, and its concept is explained at the entrance. It consists of three parts – steps, memorial stone and seats. The 50 steps, individually laid and representing the 50 American states, lead up a hill through dense woodland, left unkempt to signify the mystery and vitality of nature. After a short climb you come to the monument itself, a simple, seven-tonne slab of stone. This announces that the surrounding 0.4 hectare (1 acre) was given to the American people in memory of John Fitzgerald Kennedy, United States President from 1961 to 1963.

A quote from Kennedy's inaugural address, inscribed on the memorial, echoes the spirit of the Magna Carta: 'Let every nation know, whether it wishes us well or ill, that we shall pay any price, bear any burden, meet any hardships, support any friend or oppose any foe in order to ensure the survival and success of liberty.' JFK was, however, a master of rhetoric who managed to conceal his darker side, his deals with gangsters and constant affairs, until well after his death. A hawthorn bush, a symbol of Catholicism, stands to the left of the stone to indicate his religion, and an American scarlet oak stands behind it. By coincidence, the leaves of this tree turn red in November, the month of his assassination. A path to the right of the monument leads to simple concrete benches overlooking the meadows and river.

Through Hardship to the Stars

Follow a narrow wooded track uphill from the left corner behind the monument. This brings you out by the gate to a house, where a sealed drive continues uphill. Carry on up here, enjoying the views of the golf course on the left, part of Brunel University's grounds.

At the end of the drive, turn left and walk along the grass verge beside the busy A328 for about 50 metres (55 yards). Take the first turning on the left (Cooper's Hill Road), where you can escape from the traffic again. You are now on top of Cooper's Hill. The next stretch of the walk leading up to the RAF Memorial is on a level, paved road bordered by grand houses. These are all attractive, especially the ivy-covered Kingswood Cottage just before the memorial.

A military atmosphere greets as you enter the Air Forces Memorial. The landscape and architecture is rigidly ordered, and the lawns are neat and clipped. Despite this initial coldness, the place has a certain poignancy. The RAF motto, 'Per Ardua Ad Astra' (Through Hardship to the Stars), is blazoned across the entrance, while above this stands the figure of an eagle spreading its wings. Inside the memorial, a set of cloisters, consisting of countless pillars, records the names of airmen from Commonwealth countries who never returned from active duty during World War II. Plastic and cloth flowers add colour to the sombre scene, left by the families of sons or brothers who gave their lives for their country.

The memorial's location on top of a hill is appropriate for men whose lives were spent in the sky, and its crowning glory is the view from the top of the tower. A spiral staircase leads up from a small chapel facing an engraved window, and the vista from the top is breathtaking. Looking north, from west to east, the scene includes Windsor Castle, factory chimneys, a broad swathe of the Thames, the extensive meadows of Runnymede, several reservoirs and Heathrow Airport. Apart from the wind whistling in your ears and the roar of distant aircraft, there is silence, and it is easy to feel that you are halfway to the stars.

Down to Earth

Coming down to earth, leave the memorial, turn left and follow the road past Barn Park, a large Victorian building. The sealed road begins to dip down the hill and quickly becomes a wide, rough track. Follow the track that veers to the right under enormous beech trees, heading down the side of Cooper's Hill. Go past a house on the right (Grand View), after which the track narrows. As the road bends to the right and the view opens up on the left, you are almost down the hill again. Go through a kissing gate by a footpath sign, and walk down a sloping hill to another gate by an oak tree straight ahead.

Turn right after the gate, or, if you would like to look at Langham Pond, a Site of Special Scientific Interest (SSSI), turn left instead and walk about 100 metres (110 yards) to the end of the meadow. The pond is thick with weed and rushes, while willows grace the bank; and it is often frequented by ducks. To continue the walk, go back to the gate under the oak and follow the edge of the field. Cross a small wooden bridge, then follow a track that weaves across the large meadow. Where another track crosses it, about 30 metres (33 yards) from a signpost at the edge of the field, turn left and make for the right-hand end of a long, tall hedge that is interspersed with willows.

When you reach the hedge, follow along beside it until it turns sharp left beside a seat. Go straight ahead here across a track and towards a stile by the road. (***Walkers arriving by train*** join the walk here.) Climb over the stile, then cross the busy road with great care, and go straight ahead into the entrance of Runnymede CDC. Walk down a gravel drive to the right of a huge warehouse-type building, until you reach the riverside.

Turn left and wander upstream. You will probably see plenty of people and boats, a reminder that you are near the metropolitan sprawl of the city of London. The towpath passes the Wraysbury Skiff & Punting Club on the left, then leads back into the large, open recreation and picnic area beside the car park, which has a convenient tea shop. (***Walkers arriving by train*** should now follow the route from the start.)

Option – Savill Garden

Savill Garden, 'The Jewel of the Crown Estate', was designed by Sir Eric Savill, and named after him by George VI in 1951. Its landscaped gardens are planned to provide striking sights throughout the year. They include rhododendrons and magnolias in spring, roses and herbaceous borders in summer, gold and red maples in autumn, and conifers and holly in winter.

To get there, turn right from the car park. At the first roundabout, turn left on the A328 and go up the hill. At the top of the hill turn right into Castle Hill Road, then at the next junction, turn left into Bishopsgate Road. Branch left on to Wick Lane, and Savill Garden is beyond the Sun pub, just after a left-hand bend. There is no easy access by public transport.

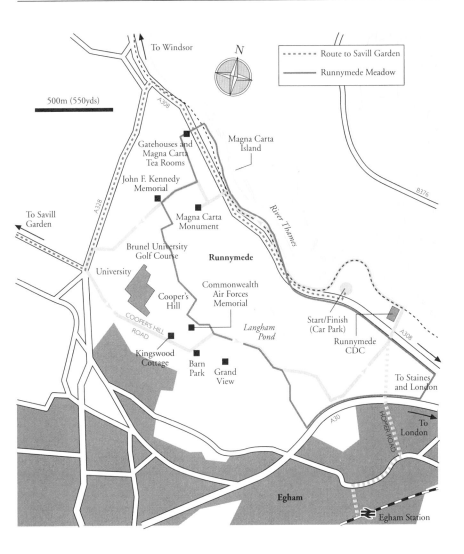

To Windsor

N

500m (550yds)

Route to Savill Garden

Runnymede Meadow

A308

Gatehouses and
Magna Carta
Tea Rooms

Magna Carta
Island

John F. Kennedy
Memorial

A328

Magna Carta
Monument

To Savill
Garden

River Thames

Brunel University
Golf Course

Runnymede

University

Cooper's
Hill

Commonwealth
Air Forces
Memorial

*Langham
Pond*

Start/Finish
(Car Park)

A308

COOPER'S HILL
ROAD

Kingswood
Cottage

Barn
Park

Grand
View

Runnymede
CDC

To Staines
and London

A30

HOMER ROAD

To
London

Egham

Egham Station

Desborough Island

Summary: In contrast to the nearby walks at Windsor, Runnymede and Hampton, this short and easy stroll has no famous castles, palaces or other monuments en route. Instead, it offers the chance to wander along country paths within an urban area. You have the river for company all the way as you skirt around an artificially created island, enjoy the varied plant life, and peek into the back gardens of riverside dwellers.

Location:	29 kilometres (18 miles) southwest of Central London.
Start/Finish:	Southwest corner of Walton Bridge. OS Explorer map 160, GR 093664.
Visitor attractions:	Scene of Caesar's Thames crossing; artificial channel on the Thames; varied plant life.
Access:	(*by car*) Walton Bridge lies on the A244 between Walton and Shepperton. Turn south into Walton Lane on the Walton side of the bridge, and pull into the car park on the left.
	(*by train*) Take a train from Waterloo to Shepperton. Leave the station and walk to the end of the road. Turn right then immediately left into Shepperton High Street. At the end of the High Street, go straight ahead at the roundabout into Church Road. Follow round a right-hand bend, then turn left into Ferry Lane, signposted 'Pedestrian Ferry'. Walk down to the riverside and cross the river by ferry (small charge). On the south bank of the river, turn left and join the walk below the first bridge across to Desborough Island.
	(*by boat*) French Brothers' boats link Shepperton Lock with Runnymede and Hampton Court. From the lock, walk east to the ferry, cross to the south bank, turn left and join walk below the first bridge across to Desborough Island.
Length:	5 kilometres (3 miles).
Time:	1.5 hours.
Refreshments:	The only refreshments available on this walk are from a kiosk opposite the car park in summer.
Footpath status:	Broad gravel path; sealed road; country paths; narrow wooded tracks.

Background

Desborough Island was created between 1930 and 1935, when the channel of Desborough Cut was dug to make this section of the river easier to navigate. The effect of digging the cut was to leave a quiet backwater for the residents of Shepperton, and to isolate a large chunk of land, part of which is used by water

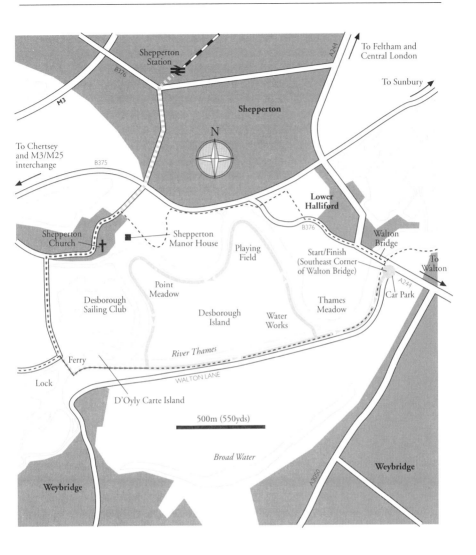

authorities, the rest of which is given over to playing fields and meadows.

The cut was named after Lord Desborough. As chairman of the Conservators of the Thames from 1904 to 1937, he was responsible for many improvements to navigation and environmental conditions on the river. Born William Henry Grenfell, he was also a true river sportsman. In the late 19th century, he was not only Amateur Punting Champion, but also rowed in the Boat Race for Oxford, sculled in a crew of three from Oxford to London in 22 hours, and rowed with an eight across the English Channel. He described this last achievement as 'a typical British feat – quite useless, exceedingly dangerous and thoroughly worthwhile'. As well as all this, he managed to serve on 115 committees at the same time.

The Walk

Colonial Crossings

Cross the road from the car park to a broad gravel path by the riverside. This stretch is popular with anglers, but is generally unremarkable. The bridge to the right is Walton Bridge, which might well qualify as the ugliest bridge on the Thames. This rusted iron structure was built as a temporary crossing several decades ago, but is still standing.

Caesar is reputed to have crossed the Thames at a fording point here, despite the water's depth of almost 2 metres (2 yards). On the opposite side, he found his progress impeded by angled stakes set into the riverbed and bank, and behind that a force of British soldiers. However, he demonstrated his powers of leadership by overcoming these obstacles, and went on from there to subjugate the nation. The scene is rather more tranquil these days, with modest yet distinctive riverside dwellings on the opposite bank. Most have conservatories or large windows facing on to the river, and many have small craft moored at the end of trim gardens.

Turn left and walk along the path towards the road bridge visible upstream. The pathway is bordered by willows and, in summer, wild flowers – willowherb, teasel and purple loosestrife. Go up the steps to the left of the bridge and pause to enjoy the view upstream, along the Desborough Cut, and downstream, towards Walton Bridge.

An Island Ramble

Follow the road on to the island. After just 100 metres (110 yards), where it branches left between buildings, keep to a track on the right by a signpost for 'Brownacres'. The river's original course lies just to the right, but the view is largely blocked by hawthorn, oak and sycamore trees.

The surroundings are rather ordinary for this part of the walk. Follow the track until it turns left by a gate marked 'Private', then carry straight on along a narrow wooded track. From here on, the dense vegetation and glimpses of the river make the walk much more enjoyable. The path follows the line of the riverbank, but a little way inland, so if you want to look at the river you need to take any of the small tracks leading off to the right. These short detours give you a view across the Thames and into the back gardens of Shepperton's riverside homes.

To the left of the main track round the island, shielded by dense shrubbery, are large playing fields for cricket and football. After a while, they give way to an area of overgrown heathland called Point Meadow. There are paths leading on to it, and you might be tempted to explore it a little further. Rabbits scuttle in the undergrowth and you may see ponies grazing; in summer, ragwort, thistles and balsam add a splash of colour.

In the northwest corner of the island, the path turns sharply to the south opposite the heart of old Shepperton village. The huge white 19th-century building surrounded by a fenced lawn is Manor House, where George Eliot (1819–80) wrote *Scenes of Clerical Life*. To the left of this is the Warren Lodge Hotel and the tower of

Shepperton Church, then to their left is the Desborough Sailing Club, which sits beside a large flooded gravel pit.

Continue on the path, which now leads to the southwest corner of the island. There are more views of the river's former course along this stretch, and more paths tempting you inland to Point Meadow. Small bays, ideal for anglers, are snuggled between the roots of riverside sycamores.

Finally, the path comes out beside another road bridge crossing back over the Desborough Cut. Looking upstream, you can see the small D'Oyly Carte Island, named after the opera impresario who lived there in the late 19th century, with Shepperton Lock beyond. On the right wall of the bridge is a plaque commemorating the opening of the cut by Lord Desborough. Walk across the bridge, go down steps to the right, then turn right to go under it. (***Walkers arriving by train*** join the walk here).

Along the Cut

From here the walk takes you along the towpath beside the river as it flows through the Desborough Cut, then back down to Walton Bridge. It is straight almost all the way, following a broad, firm track that passes between the river and a minor road. You may notice more river traffic along here than around the island, and the grassy banks make a good spot to rest if necessary. The opposite bank is thick with vegetation – towering poplars and dense hawthorns. The near bank is dotted with wild flowers in summer, including bright yellow sprays of goldenrod. Go under the road bridge (***walkers arriving by train*** should cross the bridge and follow instructions from An Island Ramble), and retrace your steps along the riverside to Walton Bridge and the car park.

Hampton Court

Summary: Second only to Windsor Castle in popularity among royals, Hampton Court Palace has been home to several kings and queens in the course of its 500-year history. The enormous building, part Tudor and part Baroque, is certainly worth exploring in its own right, and a walk around its grounds and gardens completes the impression of grandeur. This walk begins at the Lion Gate, then passes through the formal gardens of the palace before reaching the river. It goes around a huge bend, in which the river changes course from southeast to north, and finally returns through the wide-open spaces of Home Park, where deer roam freely.

Location:	24 kilometres (15 miles) southwest of Central London.
Start/Finish:	The Lion Gate, to the north of Hampton Court Palace. OS Explorer map 161, GR 157688.
Visitor attractions:	Hampton Court; Hampton Court Gardens; Home Park.
Access:	(*by car*) Hampton Court lies between Kingston and Hampton on the A308. Turn into Bushy Park opposite the Lion Gate entrance to Hampton Court Palace. Drive straight up to the Diana Fountain and park in the car park to the northeast of the fountain. Note closing time of park displayed at entrance. Walk back down to park entrance and cross the road to the Lion Gate. (*by train*) Take a train from Waterloo to Hampton Court. On leaving the station, turn right, cross the bridge and turn right again into the main entrance to the palace. If you want to visit the palace, buy your ticket on the left here. To get to the Lion Gate, go up to the main entrance, turn left in front of it and walk along past the Tiltyard Tearooms. Just beyond here, go diagonally right and walk past the maze on the left to the Lion Gate. (*by boat*) French Brothers' boats and Westminster Passenger Service link Hampton Court with places between Runnymede and Westminster.
Length:	6.5 kilometres (4 miles).
Time:	2 hours.
Refreshments:	King's Arms and Lion Gate Hotel beside Lion Gate entrance to Hampton Court; Tiltyard Tearooms in palace grounds.
Pathway status:	Country paths; gravel drives; towpath.
Best time to visit:	Bear in mind that in mid-July, Home Park is used for the Hampton Court Flower Show, when admission is charged.

Background

The land on which Hampton Court Palace now stands originally belonged to the Knights Hospitallers of St John of Jerusalem from the 13th to the 16th centuries, and was used as an administrative centre for their agricultural estates. In 1514 Thomas Wolsey, Archbishop of York and chief minister to the king, took out a 99-year lease on the place and began the expansion of what is now England's largest palace. The name most closely associated with Hampton Court is Henry VIII, who appropriated it from Wolsey in 1528. Over the next 12 years the growth continued, with hundreds of rooms being built, as well as tennis courts, bowling alleys and pleasure gardens. When Henry was host to the French ambassador in 1546, over 1,500 people were feasted and fêted for six days, and the grounds around the palace were surrounded by gold and velvet tents.

Little changed until the late 17th century, when William III commissioned Christopher Wren to rebuild the palace. His intention was to destroy almost all the former structure, but time and money proved insufficient. His insistence on rapid results led to the collapse of one section, killing two workers and injuring many others. The present-day East and South Fronts are the results of these changes. As it happened, William never lived to enjoy the fruits of his planning. He died after falling from his horse while hunting in the palace grounds in 1702.

Subsequent monarchs made minor changes to the palace, and Queen Victoria opened it to the public in 1838. The most significant event of the 20th century was a fire in 1986, which destroyed much of the King's Apartments. Restoration was completed in 1995.

The Walk

A Maze in Hampton

Facing the palace from the Lion Gate, there is a tall yew hedge on your right, and you may hear the excited shouts of children coming from behind it. This is the famous maze, originally planted in 1690, which continues to confuse and delight visitors to this day. It is only a third of an acre (0.135 hectares) in size, so it seems that getting to its heart and finding the way out should be easy. Yet most people take 20 minutes or more, retracing their steps several times, before solving the puzzle.

If you would like to visit the maze or the palace itself (admission charge for both), now is the time to do so. Follow signposts to the main entrance from the maze, and allow at least a couple of hours to see some of the main attractions: Henry VIII's Apartments, the Tudor Kitchens, the Renaissance Picture Gallery, the King's Apartments, the Queen's State Apartments and the Georgian Rooms. To see everything would take a whole day. Costumed guides are on hand to answer visitors' queries and recorded tours are also available.

To continue the walk, go diagonally left from the Lion Gate across an area known as the Wilderness, which contains many exotic trees and is covered with a carpet of bluebells and daffodils in spring. This leads to another gateway, which takes you through to the formal gardens and the East Front of the building. From this perspective, notice the sharp contrast in architectural styles between the Tudor part on the right, characterized by dark bricks and tall chimney stacks, and the Baroque part on the left, with its light bricks, huge windows and ornate stone work.

Through the Formal Gardens

Turn right and walk along the Broad Walk that passes the East Front of the building. You may find it difficult to decide whether to give more attention to the building or to the gardens, since both are equally impressive. Designed by Sir Christopher Wren, this part of the palace is probably the most famous example of Baroque architecture in England. Its stone centrepiece features a relief of *Hercules Triumphing Over Envy* by Caius Gabriel Cibber, which is set on huge Corinthian columns. The central Great Fountain Garden attracts the eye with its radiating paths, and the beautifully designed flower beds, set in immaculate lawns between yew trees, are full of vivid colours in summer. The design of the gardens has changed little since the late 17th century, when William and Mary brought in exotic plants from around the world. Over 40 gardeners are employed at Hampton Court, and this area alone must keep several of them constantly busy.

Before continuing the walk, you might like to wander around the gardens for a while, or take a horse and carriage ride around them, available in summer. You can also enjoy the view along Long Water, an artificial canal built for Charles II, which is bordered by an avenue of stately lime trees. The route will bring you back alongside this canal later.

At the end of the massive East Front is the entrance to the Privy Garden, to which there is also an admission charge. As the name suggests, this was once a private garden for the exclusive use of royalty. It has been restored to the condition it was in at the beginning of the 18th century, with patterns cut in the grass, statues and intricate flower beds. At the south end of the garden, beside the river, are the Tijou Screens, which have recently been restored. These are 12 iron gates, each with a different design of intertwined birds, flowers and heraldic shields. Beyond the Privy Garden are the Pond or Sunken Gardens, originally used as fishponds but now planted with bright flowers. At the far end of this path in a greenhouse is the Great Vine, planted by 'Capability' Brown around 1768 and believed to be the oldest vine on record in the world.

Beside the Calming River

The walk carries on along the Broad Walk, past the walls of the Privy Garden, and you can catch a small glimpse inside as it approaches the river. At the end, turn left and walk along a gravel drive beside a wall. This runs parallel to the river, which is on your right. You may well have been surrounded by crowds milling about the East Front (the gardens alone attract over a million visitors a year), but you can now leave them behind and relax.

Leave the palace grounds by a gate in the wall and continue downstream along the riverbank. Opposite is Ditton's Skiff and Punting Club, then some elaborate houses facing on to the river. The river then broadens out, creating an island near the opposite bank. This is the densely populated Thames Ditton. On the left, behind a high fence, is a golf course.

The path follows the river as it swings around to the north, and the peace is interrupted only by boats. There are several benches along the bank, where you can rest and enjoy the solitude. The unkempt appearance of the bank, scattered with ash

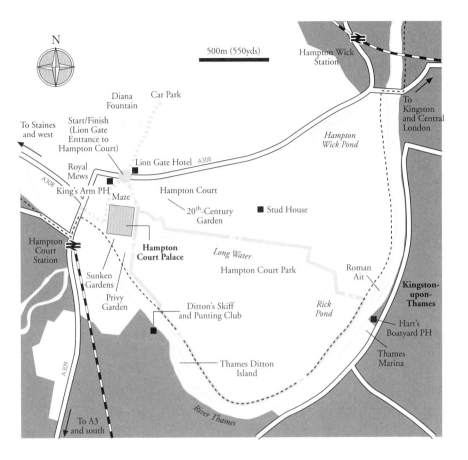

trees, shrubs and wild flowers, makes a pleasing contrast to the formality of the palace gardens. The path gets progressively overgrown as you continue, but not enough to impede your progress.

On the opposite bank, you will soon see the Thames Marina, where working barges are moored, followed by Harts' Boatyard, a pub and a restaurant. Shortly further on in the centre of the river is Ravens' Ait, an island which is presumably named after ravens living in the vicinity. As you approach this island, look out on the left for an iron gateway that leads back into the palace grounds. Go through it, walk along a path bordered by high wooden fences, and then through another gate, where the view opens up again on to a lovely pastoral scene.

Return Through Home Park

Go diagonally to the right past the end of Rick Pond. This spot is totally isolated and unspoiled, and if you are lucky, you may be able to appreciate it alone. Continue to a sealed track. Follow this along to the left until you reach a junction beside the far end of Long Water. There is a very good chance that you will see groups of fallow or red deer, of which there are hundreds in the park. These are descendants of the deer that used to be kept for hunting purposes.

Take a moment to admire the East Front of the palace in the distance, then turn right and walk beside Long Water through an avenue of lime trees. Long Water is 1,200 metres (1,300 yards) long and is frequented by herons, swans, ducks and coots. Yellow and white water lilies float on its surface, and it has a healthy population of fish. At the end, walk a little to the right and re-enter the Great Fountain Garden through a large gate. Just to the right, there is a smaller gate leading to the 20th-century garden, another very pleasant area to explore if you have time.

Once back in the Great Fountain Garden, walk around to the right of the buildings and back to the gate that you came through near the beginning of the walk, leading to the Wilderness. Retrace your steps diagonally right across to the Lion Gate, where the walk ends.

Richmond

Summary: Beginning at a peaceful spot beside Ham House, this walk follows a leafy reach of the river, then climbs through a well-laid-out park to the famous view of the Thames from Richmond Hill. From here it continues along the ridge into Richmond Park, where deer wander freely. After passing more views out to the west, the path descends and crosses Ham Common. From here it cuts through the backstreets of Ham to Teddington Lock, the last lock on the river, and returns to the start by way of a riverside ramble.

Location:	14.5 kilometres (9 miles) west of Central London.
Visitor attractions:	Ham House (option); Terrace Gardens; view from Richmond Hill; deer and views in Richmond Park; Teddington Lock.
Start/Finish:	Car park beside river at north end of Ham Street, next to Ham House. OS Explorer map 161, GR 170732.
Access:	(*by car*) Ham House lies off the A307 between Richmond and Kingston. Turn into Sandy Lane (signposted to Ham House), then go right into Ham Street. Park in the car park at the end of the road by the river.
	(*by Underground or train*) Take the District Line Underground or main line from Waterloo to Richmond. Turn left out of the station and walk along The Quadrant and George Street. Follow the main road left into Hill Street, then branch left along Hill Rise and join the walk from Richmond Hill.
	(*by boat*) Westminster Passenger Service links Richmond with places between Hampton Court and Westminster.
Length:	9.5 kilometres (6 miles); or a shorter version of 7 kilometres (4½ miles).
Time:	3½ hours (long version); 2½ hours (short version).
Refreshments:	The Roebuck on Richmond Hill; tea shop at Pembroke Lodge; Lockside snack bar at Teddington Lock (in summer).
Pathway status:	Towpath; pavements; sealed paths; gravel paths; dirt tracks.
Best time to visit:	The view from Richmond Hill is best on a sunny evening; if you start the walk in the afternoon, you can drive back up here after the walk.
Route notes:	The towpath can flood in winter. Contact the Environment Agency for information.

Background

Richmond was originally known as Shene until Henry VII renamed it in 1499. It has always been a popular place for nobles and professionals wanting to escape the city, and retains a classy atmosphere to this day. The view of the Thames from Richmond Hill has attracted and inspired a number of artists and writers, including

Sir Walter Scott, J.M.W. Turner and Charles Dickens. Richmond Park, which covers 800 hectares (2,000 acres), was enclosed by Charles I in 1637 and remains the largest public space in London, with hundreds of deer roaming in its woods.

Teddington Lock, visited near the end of the walk, marks a significant change of character in the Thames, since downstream from here it is tidal. Three separate locks cater for a variety of boats, ranging from skiffs to convoys of barges. Anywhere between 2,200 and 68,000 million litres (500 and 15,000 million gallons) of water pass through here daily on their way through Central London to the sea.

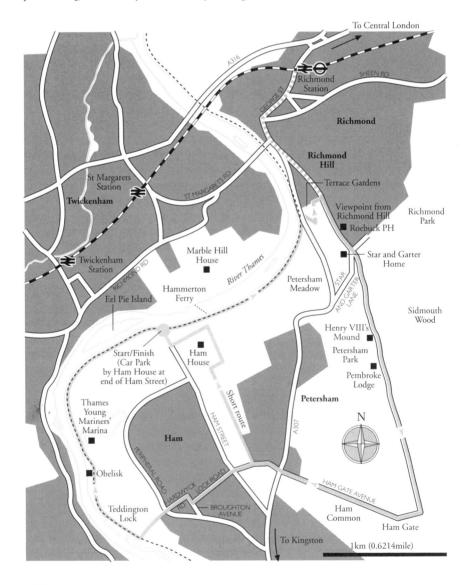

The Walk

Option – Ham House

Tucked away behind dense riverside vegetation, Ham House is one of the best examples of a 17th-century aristocratic home in the country – not only because of its architecture, but also its tapestries, paintings, furnishings and formal garden. To reach the entrance, go back down Ham Street a few steps and turn left, or alternatively turn right along the riverside, then right again through an avenue of lime trees.

The front garden sets the tone of grandeur with a statue of a River God, reminiscent of Father Thames (see page 36), with his flowing hair and robust masculinity. He has a twin that you will see shortly in Terrace Gardens. The statue is surrounded by busts of Roman emperors set in recesses in the wall and house. To the left of the house is a knot garden with box hedges trimmed into precise cones, enclosing beds of lavender and santolina. Behind the house are eight small lawns, called 'platts' (plots) and a wilderness area enclosed by hedges where wild flowers grow. To the west of the house is an orangery, which now functions as a tea room, and a rose garden.

The house itself was built in 1610, but was enlarged and lavishly decorated in the 1670s by Elizabeth, Countess of Dysart, whose insatiable ambition and political scheming enabled her to survive unscathed through the shifts of power from Charles I to Cromwell and on to Charles II. The Countess's second husband, the Duke of Lauderdale, was a member of Charles II's 'Cabal', or group of intimate advisers. They often met at Ham House, 'concocting shameful schemes for replenishing their own and their master's exchequers', as J. Penderel-Brodhurst put it in *The Royal River* (1885). Elizabeth's descendants did little to change the house, so as you wander through the dining rooms, dressing rooms and bedchambers, up the Great Staircase to the Long Gallery and library, you get a good sense of how the rich lived in the 17th century.

To the Terrace Gardens

As you face the river, turn right and walk downstream along the broad gravel towpath, where limes, chestnuts, willows and alders line both banks. Ahead, you can see the houses, hotels and rest homes that overlook the river from Richmond Hill. The path passes the boarding point for the Hammerton Ferry, one of the few remaining ferries on the Thames. On the opposite bank, just downstream of the ferry, you can catch a glimpse of Marble Hill House, a Palladian villa built in 1724–29 by George II for his mistress Henrietta Howard.

Soon you pass a slipway into the river and then the large expanse of Petersham Meadows on the right. The large building on the hill is the Star and Garter home for disabled sailors, soldiers and airmen, formerly a hotel. At the end of the meadow, the river makes a graceful sweep to the north, veering away from the hill ahead. At this point the path bends to the right, away from the river.

Just in front of some public conveniences, go left into Richmond riverside gardens. Follow the sealed path under massive plane trees, until you see three ancient archways down a few steps to your right, with eerie, crumbling faces on each pier. Go through the central arch, which leads via a subway into Terrace Gardens.

As you enter the gardens, there is a view of colourful flower beds and many unusual trees, including cedars, spruce, redwood, maidenhair, and, in the foreground to the right, an oriental plane. There is a conservatory on the left, and resting on the lawn, like his twin at Ham House, is a Coade stone River God. Five of these were made as garden ornaments by John Bacon (1740–99) and sold at 100 guineas each, but the location of the other three is unknown.

The View from Richmond Hill

You can follow any route up to the top of the gardens, but to avoid a steep climb, go to the right end and then cut back sharp left. This takes you up a gentle slope through dense trees. Take the third set of steps on the right, then go right up to Aphrodite's Fountain, a striking statue by Allan Howes (1952), set among lush reeds. Go right again behind the fountain, taking the winding path that leads out of the gardens to Richmond Hill. Turn right on to a wide paved walkway, go up another flight of steps and walk along to the viewpoint. (*Walkers arriving by train* join and leave here.)

Three boards indicate all the famous places that should be visible from here, such as Windsor Castle and Heathrow Airport. You can also see the stretch of river you have walked along, bordered by thickets of trees. When you have lingered long enough, go on to the end of Richmond Hill and the gateway to Richmond Park. On the right you pass The Wick, then Wick House. From 1772 to 1992, this was a country home of Joshua Reynolds, a great portrait painter. Walk on past the imposing façade of the Star and Garter, and notice the interesting vaulted iron structure in the middle of the road. This was presented by the Richmond RSPCA and is decorated with small dragons and large lamps.

The Keyhole Vista

Cross over Star and Garter Hill and go into Richmond Park through Richmond Gate, keeping to the sealed path on the right. Traffic does use the park, but the path veers away from it. Very soon you can enjoy the peace and quiet, along with the deer that live all around here. They are particularly numerous down the slope to your right, a continuation of the ridge of Richmond Hill.

When you reach the gate to Pembroke Lodge, go in and walk through the grounds. Pass a flower bed on the left, then go under the Laburnum Walk. Follow the left branch up on to a knoll known as Henry VIII's Mound. This mound has macabre associations, for it is where the king is said to have stood in 1536, waiting for a sign from the Tower of London that Anne Boleyn had been beheaded. A dense holly hedge blocks the view east these days, though a cleverly designed 'keyhole vista' allows a view of St Paul's Cathedral, 16 kilometres (10 miles) away.

The view westwards is another matter, and in 1727 it inspired the following words from the nature poet James Thomson, which are inscribed in a spiral on top of the mound: 'Heavens! What a goodly prospect spreads around, of hills, and dales, and woods, and lawns, and spires, and glittering towns, and gilded streams, till all the stretching landskip into smoke decays!' – a view that is still more or less accurate today.

Continue wandering southward, following the path to the right behind Pembroke House, a popular place to take tea. Walk round to the front to appreciate the columned entrance. The house was built in 1727–9 by the Earl of Pembroke. In the 19th century, Queen Victoria gave it to Lord John Russell, Prime Minister at the time. It was later the childhood home of his grandson, Bertrand Russell (1872–1970), a philosopher and writer.

The sealed path winds on a little way beyond the house. Where it bends sharply, go ahead on a narrow gravel path and through a gateway, leaving the Lodge grounds. Turn left on to the broad gravel path, then walk on southwards along Hornbeam Walk until you reach a road coming up from the right. Just before the junction, turn right on to the gravel path and follow the gentle slope down to Ham Gate, beside which there is a small pond.

Across Ham Common

Go out through the gate and straight ahead along a narrow dirt track to the right of Ham Gate Avenue. The dense woods on the left and right attract the eye, particularly the white silver birch trunks. Just after a few houses on the right that include the grand, early 18th-century Ormeley Lodge, there is a traffic light.

Cross straight over at the traffic light and follow the pavement as it bends around to the left. A residential area of Ham is on your right, and an open green on your left. If you would prefer to cut the walk short, turn right where the pavement divides, going through a white wooden fence. Go down a long, straight walk to the back gate of Ham House. Follow the path to the right and round the wall of the house to the riverside, then a few steps left to the car park.

To continue the walk, carry straight on along the pavement ahead. To the left is a classic English village scene with a pond on the green, weeping willows and Georgian houses. Cross Ham Street and go down Lock Road. For the next ten minutes the route passes the backstreets of Ham, a reminder that you are still in London. At the end of Lock Road, cross Broughton Avenue and walk about 20 metres (22 yards) to the right, then go left into a wide alley with a high wooden fence on each side. At the end, cross over Hardwycke Road and go down another path beside flats to Peripheral Road. Cross again and follow the sealed footpath down to Teddington Lock.

The Beginning of London River

The wooded area that leads down to the lock, stretching away to the right, was once full of gravel pits but was filled in with rubble from World War II bomb sites. Out of this, nature has worked a wonder and produced a habitat for over 200 species of plants. The path comes out by a footbridge to Teddington, but you turn right to reach the mechanical marvel of Teddington Lock.

Just as Oxonians call the upper reaches of the Thames the 'Isis', the stretch from here to the sea is known to Londoners as 'London River'. This is the westernmost limit of tidal influence, making Teddington a significant point in the river's changing character. The lock also signals a change in river traffic. Above Teddington, it is mostly recreational, whereas below it the boats are almost all commercial. If you have visited many locks along the river, you will immediately notice that Teddington is much more complex than all the others. There are in fact three different locks – the skiff lock (also known as the 'coffin lock'), the launch lock and the barge lock. Turn right and walk beside the barge lock. Usually only a small section of this operates, but at the end of the lock island there is another set of gates and an amazing enclosure 198 metres (215 yards) long, especially designed for a tug towing six barges.

Walk on from the lock, heading northwards through shady trees. Soon you pass a simple stone obelisk on the left. Here, plaques dated 1909 mark the point where the Port of London Authority takes over from the Thames Conservancy, now the Environment Agency. From here, bushes and trees line the path, an occasional gap allowing views of the houses and boatyards on the opposite bank. Soon after the Thames Young Mariners' Marina, the path begins to turn gently westwards.

On the left, you approach the large Eel Pie Island with small properties perched on its banks. Its name is a cultural throwback: the Thames used to teem with eels, and they were once a popular food. As the path passes the end of the island, you suddenly see the grand houses of Richmond Hill, straight ahead along the river. Diagonally to the right is Ham House, and in front of you, with luck, is your car.

Barnes and Fulham

Summary: Though not far from the centre of London, much of the path on this walk is bordered by bushes and towering trees. You pass a huge Wetland Centre, then the sailing and rowing clubs on the bank at Putney, the starting point for the annual Oxford–Cambridge Boat Race. On the return leg, you can take time to explore Fulham Palace Gardens, 'London's best-kept secret', and, if you are a Fulham supporter, bow before Craven Cottage, Fulham's football ground.

Location:	8 kilometres (5 miles) from Central London.
Start/Finish:	North side of Hammersmith Bridge. OS Explorer map 161, GR 782230.
Visitor attractions:	Hammersmith Bridge; Wetland Centre (option); starting point of Boat Race; Bishop's Park; Fulham Palace Gardens.
Access:	(*by car*) Make your way to Hammersmith roundabout, which surrounds the bus and tube station. Take the minor exit on the left just before Hammersmith Church, in front of the London Apollo (St Catherine's Road). Turn immediately right and park in the Pay & Display car park under the flyover. Walk to the far end of the car park, turn left into Hammersmith Bridge Road and walk down to the bridge.
	(*by Underground*) Go to Hammersmith, then follow signs for Hammersmith Bridge Road. Walk down to the bridge.
Length:	6.5 kilometres (4 miles).
Time:	2½ hours.
Refreshments:	Several pubs on the riverside near Hammersmith and Putney bridges (perhaps the most authentic is The Dove, upstream from Hammersmith Bridge – not on the route of the walk); refreshment stall in Bishop's Park just outside Fulham Palace Gardens (in summer).
Pathway status:	Towpath; pavements; sealed paths.
Best time to visit:	If you don't like crowds, avoid Boat Race day or Saturday afternoons when Fulham football team is playing at home.

Background

These last few walks are beside the tidal Thames, where the river's character is radically different. When the tide is out, it appears almost a distant stranger from the high banks; when it is in, it surges past with awesome power, and in parts its flow is extremely wide.

The walk crosses two of London's bridges, all of which add character to the river and city. They link north and south London, almost different cities – the north is brash and glitzy compared with the workaday, bustling south. Until the 18th century,

London Bridge was the only route across the river, which helps to explain the difference. The contrast is less evident around Barnes and Fulham, both desirable addresses for city dwellers.

Hammersmith, where the walk begins, was the last home (1890–96) of the Victorian writer, designer and printer William Morris. Kelmscott House faces the Thames a few steps upstream from The Dove pub (see Refreshments). It was named after Morris' idyllic Elizabethan manor in Kelmscot, near the source of the Thames (see page 42).

The Walk

A Country Stroll in the City

Begin the walk by crossing to the south bank over Hammersmith suspension bridge. Notice the elaborate designs on the ironwork and the date (1887). The bridge was designed by Sir Joseph Bazalgette, one of the Thames' 19th-century heroes. As well as bridge-building, he is renowned for constructing the Embankment in Central London, and for his installation of a sewage system. This finally ended the Great Stink, which, in the mid-19th century, caused sessions of parliament to be suspended at times.

At the end of the bridge turn sharp left, go down to the riverbank and turn right to begin a relaxing saunter downstream. You are immediately surrounded by grassy banks and tall, overhanging trees. On the right, after passing some apartment buildings set back from the path, you will see the solid façade of Harrod's Depository, with distinctive domes on its roof. After more apartments, you will reach a long stretch bordered by former reservoirs. These have been converted into a Wetland Centre for wildfowl. If you want to visit the centre, for which there is an admission charge, turn right along Queen Elizabeth's Walk and walk about 1.5 kilometres (1 mile) to the entrance.

Option – Wetland Centre

Artist and naturalist Sir Peter Scott (1909–89) always dreamed of a sanctuary for wildfowl within London, and it has eventually come about through the Wildfowl & Wetlands Trust, which he founded in 1946. The Wetland Centre, opened in 2000, covers 40 hectares (100 acres), and includes a main lake, a reed bed, a grazing marsh, a wader scrape and a sheltered lagoon. These habitats are designed to attract a wide range of birds, such as herons, reed warblers, lapwings, sandpipers, goldeneyes and shovelers; and with its two- and three-storey hides and an observatory, it is a birdwatcher's heaven. There is also a visitor centre, a restaurant, café and shop.

Starting Point of the Boat Race

Continue your walk downstream, looking down towards Putney Bridge where the floodlights of Fulham football ground rise high above the buildings on the left. Soon the path passes Wandsworth and South Bank sailing clubs, the first of many along this bank, with a slipway down to the river. Depending on the time of year, you may see sailing dinghies bobbing on the water and rowing crews practising for their next event. From here on, the opposite bank is lined with a long promenade

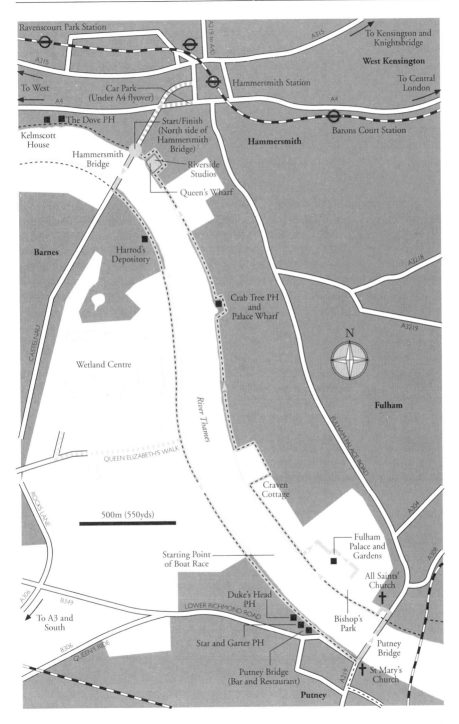

Ravenscourt Park Station

A315

A219 to A40

A315

To Kensington and Knightsbridge

West Kensington

To West

A4

Hammersmith Station

To Central London

A4

Car Park (Under A4 flyover)

Barons Court Station

The Dove PH

Start/Finish (North side of Hammersmith Bridge)

Hammersmith

Kelmscott House

Hammersmith Bridge

Riverside Studios

Queen's Wharf

A3218

Barnes

Harrod's Depository

Crab Tree PH and Palace Wharf

A3219

N

CASTELNAU

Wetland Centre

River Thames

Fulham

QUEEN ELIZABETH'S WALK

Craven Cottage

FULHAM PALACE ROAD

ROCKS LANE

500m (550yds)

Fulham Palace and Gardens

A304

A308

All Saints' Church

Starting Point of Boat Race

A306

B349

Duke's Head PH

Bishop's Park

To A3 and South

B306

QUEEN'S RIDE

LOWER RICHMOND ROAD

Star and Garter PH

Putney Bridge

Putney Bridge (Bar and Restaurant)

A219

St Mary's Church

Putney

of enormous plane trees that you will pass under on your way back.

The towpath ends at a small bridge over a Thames tributary. After this, the path follows the pavement beside the Embankment down to Putney Bridge. You soon pass a very wide slipway, leading up to a cluster of sailing and rowing clubs – Thames, Vesta, Ranelagh, Westminster School and many others. This is the starting point of the famous Oxford–Cambridge Boat Race, which has taken place every spring since the mid-19th century, except for during the world wars. The race ends at Chiswick Bridge in Mortlake.

There are some pubs just before Putney Bridge: the Duke's Head, the Star and Garter and Putney Bridge, a modern, boat-shaped bar and restaurant. A barge-loading slipway juts into the river, once a bustling scene but now quite idle. For the final few steps up to the bridge, the Embankment meets up with the Lower Richmond Road. Just beyond the bridge, notice the tower of the Church of St Mary the Virgin set against the background of a modern glass building, forming a striking contrast in architectural styles.

It is common for bridges over the Thames to be flanked by inns or pubs, as they offered welcome refreshment in the days when travel both by river and road was slow and wearing. Putney Bridge, however, has a church on either side – St Mary's on the south and All Saints' on the north. There was a ferry in operation here before a wooden bridge was built in 1729. The bridge you see today dates from 1884. Like Hammersmith bridge, it was designed by Bazalgette, though it is much simpler and more functional.

Into Bishop's Park

Cross the bridge, then on the far side go down the steps to the left. These take you into Bishop's Park. The park was once part of Fulham Palace, but this part became public in 1921. The first small square contains some intriguing statues, portraying Adoration, Protection, Affection and Grief, as well as Leda and the Swan. Beyond this is a rose garden, and a plaque in memory of members of the International Brigade who were killed trying to prevent Franco's fascist forces from taking power during the 1930s' Spanish Civil War.

Go down to the riverside and walk upstream along the glorious broad promenade you saw earlier. The towering plane trees form a natural archway, their boughs sometimes bending down to touch the river itself. With its maple-like leaves and smooth but flaking bark, the London Plane is a common feature of all London's parks and leafy avenues. Outside the city, it is seen much less.

Discovering 'London's Best-kept Secret'

About halfway along this lovely walkway, you will see a play area and pools on the right. If you would like to take a look at Fulham Palace Gardens (highly recommended), turn right here and follow signposts. The gardens are free but there is a small charge for the museum (see Opening Times). The gardens are appropriately tagged 'London's best-kept secret', and are rarely crowded, even in the height of summer.

If you are expecting a building to rival Hampton Court, you will be disappointed,

Plate 23: Spring brings new colour to Magna Carta Island in Runnymede (see page 112).

Plate 24: The sloping banks of Savill Garden are beautifully landscaped (see page 114).

Plate 25: Well-appointed house on the quiet waters at Shepperton (see page 118).

Plate 26: Viewed from across the formal gardens, the south and east wings of Hampton Court Palace. Both of these sections were rebuilt in the 17th century by Christopher Wren (see page 120).

Plate 27: One of the most celebrated views in the southeast: early evening light over the Thames from the top of Richmond Hill (see page 125).

Plate 28: Herb garden and remains of glasshouse at Fulham Palace Gardens – 'London's best-kept secret' (see page 131).

Plate 29: Statue of Leda and the Swan in Bishop's Park Gardens (see page 134).

Plate 30: Reconstruction of Sir Francis Drake's Golden Hinde (see page 139).

Plate 31: The Millennium Dome on the banks of the Thames at Greenwich (see page 149).

Plate 32: The Royal Naval College and Queen's House seen from the Thames Path (see page 147).

Plate 33: The mighty Thames Barrier marks the end of the official Thames Path (see page 149).

as the term 'palace' was traditionally used to describe a bishop's residence. This one was a summer retreat for over a hundred bishops of London between 704 and 1973. Nevertheless, this is an admirable Grade 1 listed building, consisting of a Tudor court-yard and a Georgian extension in which the museum is housed. The chapel was added in 1866, and the Coachman's Lodge, just to the left of the imposing gateposts at the entrance, in 1898. The site was once surrounded by a moat over 1.5 kilometres (1 mile) long. The museum displays the results of archaeological digs, which uncovered prehistoric and Roman settlements on the site. It also contains information about the lives of a number of bishops who lived here, and a fragment of the Porteus library, complete with ancient tomes on the shelves. As well as organizing exhibitions, the museum provides educational facilities and guided tours.

The 5 hectares (13 acres) of grounds that make up the Palace Gardens are planted with many unusual and exotic species. This tradition was begun in the 17th century by Bishop Compton, an avid horticulturalist, who among other things was responsible for the introduction of magnolias to England. Don't miss the walled kitchen garden, where a wisteria pergola creates a riot of colour in spring, and a herb garden stands beside the crumbling frame of a greenhouse that once housed the vinery. Benches are scattered around the main garden so that you can sit and absorb the scene at leisure.

A Temple to England's New Religion

Retrace your steps to the riverside and turn right to continue upstream beneath the planes. When you reach the end of the promenade, turn right and walk to the gateway leading out of Bishop's Park into Stevenage Road. Turn left and walk past the long front of Craven Cottage, home of Fulham Football Club. Established in 1880, the ground attracts thousands of visitors every Saturday to watch what some would term the new religion of modern England – football.

At the end of the football ground, turn left and go down an alleyway back to the river. From here the buildings on the right are an odd mix of modern flats, terraced houses, converted wharves and offices, while on the left the river flows by, at least 100 metres (110 yards) wide at this point. Two more short diversions away from the river are necessary before arriving at Hammersmith Bridge, but both are clearly signposted to the Thames Path. The first goes around the Crab Tree pub and Palace Wharf, while the second skirts the grounds of the Riverside Studios and Queen's Wharf. The Riverside has a cinema that shows art-house and classic films, such as the works of Fellini and Buñuel (for information about their current programme, call 0208 237 1111). Once back at the riverfront by Queen's Wharf, you are a stone's throw from Hammersmith Bridge. There, continue under the bridge for a riverside drink or to look at Kelmscott House; turn right to return to the car park or under-ground station.

Central London

Summary: Going from Westminster Bridge to London Bridge and back, this route is so densely lined with places of interest that it would take several days to explore them fully. Sharks and stingrays, film stars and footballers, cathedrals and theatres – all these and more await you. This guide gives an overview of the museums and concert halls on the South Bank, the galleries and theatres of Bankside, and the impressive architecture and gardens along the Victoria Embankment.

Location: Central London.

Start/Finish: The northeast corner of Westminster Bridge, beside the South Bank Lion. OS Explorer map 173, GR 308804.

Visitor attractions: Houses of Parliament; FA Premier League Hall of Fame; London Aquarium; London Eye; Royal Festival Hall; IMAX cinema; National Theatre; Tate Gallery of Modern Art; Millennium Bridge; Globe Theatre; Vinopolis; Clink Prison Museum; Southwark Cathedral; St Paul's Cathedral; Victoria Embankment Gardens.

Access: (*by car*) (Note: Parking in Central London is very expensive.) Park in the car park beside Hungerford Bridge, between Westminster and Waterloo bridges on the south side of the river. Leaving the car park, turn right on Belvedere Road, then go right again to the northeast corner of Westminster Bridge. Alternatively, walk through to the riverfront from the car park, turn right and join the walk at the Royal Festival Hall.

(*by Underground*) Westminster Tube (Circle, District, Jubilee Lines). Turn left out of the Tube station and cross the Victoria Embankment to the northwest corner of Westminster Bridge. Walk across the bridge to the northeast corner.

Length: 6.5 kilometres (4 miles).

Time: 2½ hours (not including stops).

Refreshments: Several riverside pubs; cafés at most attractions; bars and restaurants at Gabriel's Wharf; tea house in Embankment Gardens by Temple Station.

Pathway status: Pavements.

Best time to visit: Start early in the day if you want to visit several of the attractions mentioned.

Background

The many attractions on the banks will almost certainly distract you from the surging, silent waters of the Thames along this walk, but try to remember that without the river, there would be no city here at all. It seems likely that the city's first inhabitants lived in the area around London Bridge, where the Romans first established a crossing of the river. The huge growth of the city was a direct result of London's convenient location as a port, though today commercial vessels use harbours to the east of the city. Most boats in the centre are now used to transport tourists, or as floating pubs and restaurants.

The Walk

At England's Heart

As you stand at the edge of Westminster Bridge, there are reminders on all sides that you are at the heart of England. To the west is the huge tower of Big Ben, which has kept time for the whole country since it was erected in 1858. Beside it are the Gothic walls of the Houses of Parliament, designed by Sir Charles Barry, which were completed in 1860. On the northwest corner of the bridge is a statue of Boadicea and her daughters in a chariot, sculpted by Thomas Thornycroft and erected in 1902. Boadicea, Queen of the Iceni tribe, led a revolt against the Romans in AD 60, and was one of England's earliest heroines. The bridge is a popular spot for tourists to pose for photos, and this view is just one of the attractions for the 30 million people who visit London each year.

Along the Queen's Walk

To visit the FA Premier League Hall of Fame, walk away from the bridge, go straight past the South Bank Lion and enter County Hall on the left. The Hall of Fame takes visitors on a tour of football history, from medieval days to the founding of the Football Association in 1863 and England's World Cup victory in 1966. There are also realistic models of today's top stars.

If football is not your scene, go down the steps by the riverside to walk past the front of County Hall with its neo-Renaissance colonnaded façade in the form of a crescent. From 1922 to 1986, this was the home of London's government (the Greater London Council). As well as the Football Hall of Fame, the building now houses a hotel, fast-food restaurants, a video arcade and the London Aquarium, one of the best of the South Bank's many attractions. Here, you can watch sharks and piranhas being fed, see the varied Pacific, Atlantic and Indian Ocean tanks, or even stroke a stingray.

The broad promenade running from here to Blackfriars Bridge is known as the Queen's Walk. Following World War II, this whole area was derelict wasteland, but now it boasts some of London's top attractions. Just beyond County Hall is the London Eye, an enormous ferris wheel that allows visitors to look down over the city from a height of 135 metres (433 feet). Set back behind Jubilee Gardens is the Shell Centre, a 25-storey monument to commerce rising above the cultural centres by the river.

Hungerford Railway Bridge carries thousands of commuters across the river to and from Charing Cross Station. The new footbridges on either side of it provide a convenient route from the West End to Waterloo Station; after decades of priorizing motorized transport, city planners are finally taking walkers into account. The Millennium Bridge, which the walk passes a little later, is another example of this.

Beyond Hungerford Bridge sits a mass of concrete architecture that contains one of England's prime cultural centres. The Royal Festival Hall, built for the Festival of Britain in 1951 with the sole purpose of providing top-quality acoustics, is an ideal location to enjoy a concert. The ground floor has a bookshop, a CD store and a bar, where musicians provide free entertainment at lunchtime. Beside the Festival Hall are the Queen Elizabeth Hall and Purcell Room, used for smaller musical and theatrical events. Behind these, in ascending layers of concrete, is the Hayward Gallery, which features fine art exhibitions.

There are two interesting locations for cinema lovers near Waterloo Bridge, under which the walk now passes. The National Film Theatre, with its café looking out on to the walkway, shows international classics on its two screens. A little further back from the river on the roundabout in front of Waterloo Station is the BFI IMAX cinema, which has Britain's biggest-ever screen (five London buses high!). Here, you can sit back, put on a pair of 3D glasses, and join the action.

Back on the riverfront, another concrete structure rises up in horizontal layers. This is the Royal National Theatre, which opened in 1976. The complex contains three auditoriums – the Olivier, the Lyttelton and the Cottesloe, which present a wide variety of classics, new plays and musicals. As with the Festival Hall, you can browse in the bookshops, have a coffee and enjoy free music in the foyer.

After all this concrete and culture, the small, human scale of Gabriel's Wharf, a couple of minutes' walk along the riverfront, comes as a pleasant surprise. Here, restaurants, bars and craft shops snuggle around a square; and the Bernie Spain Gardens, which you come to next, have green grass and benches where you can stop and rest.

Carry on to the famous art deco Oxo Tower, one of the few landmarks to have survived the rebuilding of the South Bank. If you avoided surveying the city from the London Eye, there is a public viewing gallery on its top floor that offers a fine panorama of London's rooftops, although it is not as high as the Eye.

Just before Blackfriars Bridge the path passes the Doggett's Coat and Badge pub. Since the early 18th century, an annual single-skulls race has taken place between watermen, a dwindling group of skilled boatmen who still make their living on the Thames; this pub was named after the prize awarded to the winner.

Bankside Made Good

Once under the road and rail bridges at Blackfriars, you are walking on Bankside, which has undergone radical transformation in recent years. First you pass the Bankside Gallery, where exhibitions of watercolours and etchings are held. You then arrive at the enormous Tate Modern art gallery, which was converted from the shell of a former power station. Directly in front of the gallery, the Millennium Bridge spans the river, allowing walkers to cross to the north bank immediately in front of St Paul's Cathedral. This walk continues a little further, up to London Bridge, but if you are running short of energy or time you could cross here, or indeed at any bridge, and begin the return leg of the walk.

Bankside was once notorious for its lowlife, which included taverns, brothels and playhouses, showing plays by the likes of Shakespeare and his contemporaries. One of these playhouses, the Globe Theatre, has now been reconstructed as faithfully as possible on a site very near the 17th-century original, and has proved to be one of London's most popular attractions. It is constructed of timber, plaster and thatch, and is the first thatched building to be built in London since the Great Fire of 1666. The permanent exhibition recreates the world of Shakespeare's day, and the theatre itself offers an experience of drama as Elizabethans knew it. If you do not enter the building, note at least the intricate designs on the gates as you pass.

Continue under Southwark Bridge and follow the riverside to The Anchor, an 18th-century pub with several cosy bars. From here the path moves away from the river, then goes left under the railway from Cannon Street. If you want to visit Vinopolis ('city of wine'), it is situated on the corner by the bridge. Here you can go on a 'Wine Odyssey' through 20 themed rooms. It also has an art gallery and restaurant.

The narrow lane beyond the railway is Clink Street, where the Clink Prison Museum offers a horrifying glimpse of prison life as it used to be in the bad old days. The name lives on in the slang expression 'in the clink', meaning in prison. Leg chains, foot crushers and other instruments of torture show what a nightmare life could be for those who fell foul of the law. The area was once full of 'stews', which functioned as bathhouses and brothels. Ironically, these were under the protection of the Bishops of Winchester, who grew fat on their profits. Just past the museum are the remains of Winchester Abbey, where a crumbling, 14th-century rose window frames the sky.

Go to the end of Clink Street, where a reproduction of the *Golden Hinde*, Sir Francis Drake's famous ship, sits in a tiny dock. Turn right and follow the road around to the entrance of Southwark Cathedral, which occupies a rare corner of calm amid the bustle of the city. Southwark is one of the oldest parts of London, and it is believed that a church has stood here since the 7th century. The oldest part of the current building, the north transept, dates back to 1206 and can be seen just inside the main entrance. The cathedral has beautiful stained glass windows, memorials to many famous people including Shakespeare, and a chapel dedicated to John Harvard. Harvard was baptized here in 1607, and later emigrated to Massachusetts. When he died, he left his books and property to the college now known as Harvard University.

Go on through the grounds of the cathedral, up the steps to the busy main road, then left and over London Bridge. If you can, try to imagine how this area might have been when people first settled here, almost 2,000 years ago. These days, it is one of the most highly developed areas in the country; the glass buildings directly in front as you cross the river belong to the banks and financial companies of the City of London. When the word 'City' is capitalized, it refers to an area of about 2.5 square kilometres (1 square mile) where the major financial institutions are concentrated, rather than the entire metropolitan area.

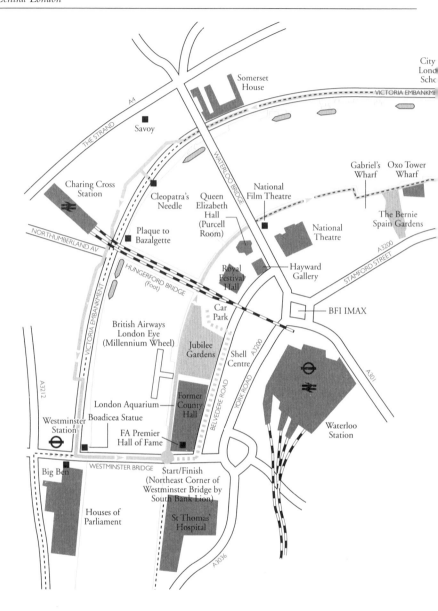

Back along the King's Reach

Go down the steps on the north bank and follow a subway to Upper Thames Street. Turn left, following signs for Thames Path West, and walk past Fishmongers Hall, which has occupied this site since 1434. Turn left down Swan Lane and go back to the river, where you will find Regalia, the first of many floating bars and restaurants along the north bank. Turn right and follow the riverside path along to Cannon

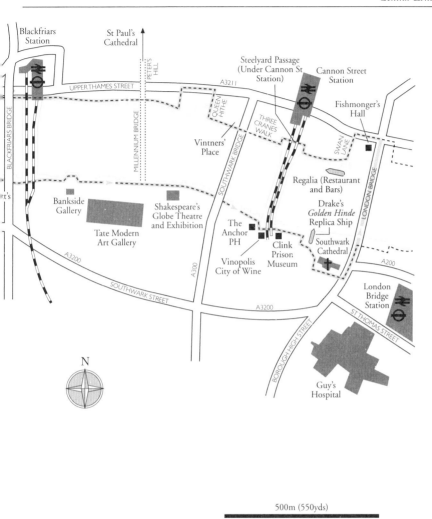

Blackfriars Station

St Paul's Cathedral

Steelyard Passage (Under Cannon St Station)

Cannon Street Station

Fishmonger's Hall

UPPER THAMES STREET

A3211

PETER'S HILL

QUEEN HITHE

THREE CRANES WALK

SWAN LANE

MILLENNIUM BRIDGE

BLACKFRIARS BRIDGE

SOUTHWARK BRIDGE

LONDON BRIDGE

Vintners' Place

Regalia (Restaurant and Bars)

Drake's *Golden Hinde* Replica Ship

Bankside Gallery

Shakespeare's Globe Theatre and Exhibition

The Anchor PH

Southwark Cathedral

Tate Modern Art Gallery

Clink Prison Museum

A3200

A300

Vinopolis City of Wine

A200

SOUTHWARK STREET

A3200

London Bridge Station

ST THOMAS STREET

N

BOROUGH HIGH STREET

Guy's Hospital

500m (550yds)

Street Station. Turn right again, then after a few paces turn left along Steelyard Passage. This passes under the station and leads into Cousins Lane.

Turn left into Cousin Lane, then right beside The Banker pub into Three Cranes Walk. This section provides a sharp contrast to the broad path and public attractions of the South Bank; the walkway here is narrow and most of the buildings belong to private companies. However, there are some interesting juxtapositions of ancient and modern architecture, and you can look back across the river at landmarks such as the Globe and the Tate.

There is a container crane along here, which may block the path for 10–15 minutes if it is operating. If so, you can either wait, or walk round the block. Continue along to Southwark Bridge, go up the steps, cross the road with care and go down the steps on the other side. The path here is called Three Barrels Walk, and passes the offices of Vintners Place. Turn right and go up a cobbled lane called Queenhithe. Turn left and briefly follow the busy road (Upper Thames Street), then turn left into Broken Wharf. From here the path stays beside the river until you reach Westminster.

If you would like to visit St Paul's Cathedral, turn right up Peter's Hill at Millennium Bridge. St Paul's is Sir Christopher Wren's masterpiece, and one of London's best-known landmarks. As with Southwark, a church existed on the site as early as the 7th century, but the cathedral we see today was built to replace the one destroyed by the Great Fire of 1666. It was completed in 1711. The grand scale of the cathedral is breathtaking, though its most distinctive feature is the cupola, a new feature in English church design at the time, and introduced by Wren. The interior of the dome is painted with scenes from the life of St Paul. You can go up to the Whispering Gallery to experience its extraordinary acoustics, and if you are feeling fit, on up to the Stone Gallery for great views of the city and the river.

Back at the riverside, continue walking upstream under both bridges at Blackfriars, then climb the steps up to the Victoria Embankment. Looking back, you can see a statue of Queen Victoria at the start of the road bridge, and the top of St Paul's, just visible above other buildings. The City of London School, on the opposite side of the road, has ornate stonework and statues of Bacon, Shakespeare, Milton and Newton along the top.

Walk down towards Waterloo Bridge, passing two silver and red dragons that mark the boundary of the City. In 1935, this stretch was named 'The King's Reach' to celebrate 25 years of rule by George V, and you pass a huge water gate commemorating this. The massive façade of Somerset House, built in the 18th century, looms on the right as you approach and go under Waterloo Bridge. Beyond the bridge, cross the road into Victoria Embankment Gardens in front of the Savoy Hotel.

An Unusual Monument

The gardens are green and peaceful with many statues of notables, such as the Scottish poet Robert Burns (1759–96), and a well-positioned tea house in case you need refreshment. Out on the riverbank, almost in front of the tea house, is Cleopatra's Needle, guarded by two giant sphinxes. This pink granite obelisk, nearly 25 metres (70 feet) high, is by far the oldest monument on the walk, dating back some 3,500 years. It was given to Britain in 1819, as a mark of gratitude for Nelson's victory over the French in the Battle of the Nile (1798). However, due to administrative and logistical delays, it did not arrive in England until 1877. In World War I it was nearly destroyed, as you can see from the gouged marks around the bases of its guardian sphinxes. Fortunately it survived, and is still one of the city's most incongruous landmarks. To add to this exotic companion of the Thames, raised benches along the broad promenade by the river are supported by strange, winged creatures, and the street lamps are adorned with writhing dolphins.

A little further along, in front of Embankment Underground Station, is a plaque to the memory of Sir Joseph Bazalgette, the chief engineer of the Victoria Embankment project. Executed between 1864 and 1870, the work not only reclaimed 37 acres of land (along which the road and gardens are now situated), but also relieved London of the unbearable stench caused by the open sewers, which emptied into the Thames. The sewers now run under the Embankment. The gardens continue between Hungerford Bridge and Westminster, with benches protected from the noisy traffic by dense vegetation. Once back at Westminster Bridge, you are right beside Westminster Pier, from where river trips go upstream to Kew, Richmond or Hampton, or downstream to Greenwich, the subject of this book's last walk.

Greenwich

Summary: This walk begins with a short stroll beside the majestic Thames as it winds northward round the Greenwich Peninsula. Turning away from the river, you then enter Greenwich Park, climb up to a viewpoint over the city and wander through relaxing flower gardens. On the return to the river, the route passes the Prime Meridian at the Old Royal Observatory, where you can learn the story of Time, and then the National Maritime Museum, which brings to life the journeys of great explorers of the past. By contrast, the optional visits to the Millennium Dome and the Thames Barrier are reminders of what modern technology can achieve.

Location:	8 kilometres (5 miles) southeast of Central London.
Start/Finish:	Cutty Sark Gardens, beside Greenwich Pier. OS Explorer map 161, GR 383779.
Visitor attractions:	The *Cutty Sark*; Royal Naval College; riverside views; city views; Old Royal Observatory; National Maritime Museum; Queen's House; Greenwich Crafts Market; Millennium Dome (option); Thames Barrier (option).
Access:	(*by car*) Enter Greenwich from New Cross on Greenwich High Road (A206), and continue on Greenwich Church Street to the end. As you approach the *Cutty Sark*, take the last turn on the left and then go down a ramp on the right to the Pay & Display car park below Cutty Sark Gardens.
	(*by train*) Take the train from Charing Cross or London Bridge to Greenwich. Turn left out of the station and follow Greenwich High Road as it bends left into Greenwich Church Street. Follow this down to Cutty Sark Gardens.
	(*by Underground*) Take the Docklands Light Railway from Bank Station to Cutty Sark, which brings you out next to Greenwich Pier and the *Cutty Sark* itself.
	(*by boat*) Take a boat from Westminster, Charing Cross, or Tower Pier to Greenwich.
Length:	6.5 kilometres (4 miles).
Time:	2½ hours.
Refreshments:	The Trafalgar Tavern and Cutty Sark pubs with views over the river; several cafés and refreshment kiosks in Greenwich park; pubs and restaurants in Greenwich.
Pathway status:	Pavements; sealed paths.

Background

Greenwich Park is the oldest royal park, having been established in 1433. However, the layout that you see today, occupying an area of 75 hectares (185 acres), dates from around 1662–5 when it was remodelled by Charles II. It has been open to the public since 1705. Charles II was fascinated by astronomy, and appointed John Flamsteed as Astronomer Royal with the specific task of determining a method for calculating longitude. The story of this quest is revealed in the Old Royal Observatory, built in 1675–6 by Sir Christopher Wren.

The only building that remains from before the remodelling is the Queen's House, designed by Inigo Jones and completed in 1638. This was the first example of the classical style, which dominated English architecture for the next 200 years. In the early 18th century, Greenwich Hospital, later to become the Royal Naval College, was built between the Queen's House and the river. However, Mary II gave instructions for the view from the house down to the Thames to be preserved, and it can still be appreciated today. The other significant building in the park is the National Maritime Museum, which was built in 1806 as a Naval Asylum, a school for the children of seamen. It assumed its present role in 1937, and has recently been expanded and modernized.

The Walk

From One Hemisphere to Another

The walk begins with a view of the *Cutty Sark*, the fastest clipper ever to sail the seas, and symbol of the explosion of trade that accompanied the growth of the British Empire. It is made of teak, weighs almost 1,000 tonnes and has a sail area of nearly 3,000 square metres (3580 square yards). Built in 1869, it carried tea from China in the 1870s, then wool from Australia in the 1880s and 90s, leaving steamers in its wake as it covered more than 350 miles a day.

For a fee, you can walk on the decks and look at the impressive collection of ships' figureheads in the hold below. The ship's name means 'short shirt' and comes from Robert Burns' poem 'Tam O'Shanter'. The boat's figurehead, Nannie the witch, comes from the same poem. A smaller and more recent slice of history stands nearby in the shape of *Gypsy Moth IV*, in which Sir Francis Chichester sailed around the world single-handed in 1966–7.

If you would like to look at the Royal Naval College, of which only the Painted Hall and Upper Hall are open to the public, the entrance is just up King William Walk beside the *Cutty Sark*. As might be expected, these rooms contain paintings glorifying William and Mary, who sat on the throne at the time of its construction, and other members of royalty.

From the north end of King William Walk, facing Greenwich Pier, turn right and walk past the huge façade of the Royal Naval College. It stands on the site of former Tudor Palace of Placentia, and was built in stages by Inigo Jones, Sir Christopher Wren and finally Sir John Vanbrugh, whose house you will pass later in the walk.

After passing the college, bear right past the entrance to the Trafalgar Tavern, a 19th-century haunt of politicians and writers such as Dickens, then turn immediately left down the alley beside the pub. Pass The Yacht pub and a terrace of Georgian and modern houses, then re-emerge by the river in front of Trinity Hospital. You can get a glimpse of its grounds through the gateway and arch, and a plaque states that it has served as a home for 21 retired gentlemen of Greenwich since 1617. A stone inscription opposite the gate records an 'exceptionally high tide' in 1928, which swept away a large section of the wall. It was to prevent such disasters that the Thames

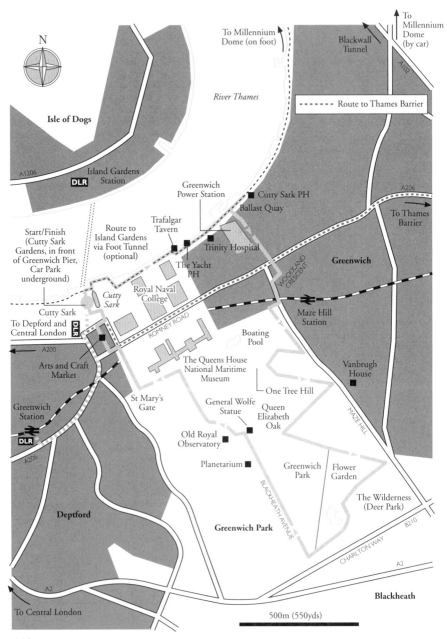

Barrier (see page 151) was built a short way downstream.

Continue on the path under the ugly metal rigging of Greenwich Power Station, past the end of Hoskins Street and Lassell Street, and on to Ballast Quay. Though there are no bright lights or notices to inform you, you have just crossed the Prime Meridian from the western to the eastern hemisphere, where you will remain until reaching the Old Royal Observatory. Ballast Quay is a cobbled street with attractive terraced houses and the Cutty Sark pub, a listed building that dates from about 1695. There is a fine view from the terrace opposite the pub towards Blackwall Reach. On the horizon, two of London's most modern landmarks flank the Thames – Canary Wharf Tower on the left, the tallest building in the country, and the Millennium Dome on the right, the largest dome in the world.

A Stroll in Greenwich Park

Retrace your steps to Lassell Street and walk down it to the end. Cross the busy Trafalgar Road with care, then go straight ahead and follow Woodland Crescent as it bends to the right. Turn left on to Maze Hill, then cross over and take the first right into Park Vista. Cross over and enter Greenwich Park by the gate near the corner, then follow the broad path up the hill to the left by a high wall.

Where the path begins to climb steeply, by the first gateway on the left, turn right along a level path for about 100 metres (110 yards), then go left up a stairway. This will bring you to the summit of One Tree Hill, a promontory with fine views over the Naval College, the Maritime Museum and river to the skyscrapers of London. The view is partly shielded by trees, but this is a quieter place than the nearby observatory, which can be rather crowded. This was one of Elizabeth I's favourite spots, according to a poem engraved on the benches here.

To see everything of interest in Greenwich Park, you need to walk in a zigzag. Turn left from the top of the steps that you came up, and walk along a level path to Maze Hill Gate. The imposing mansion just outside the park is Vanbrugh House, home of the architect who built part of the Royal Naval College. Turn right and head back towards the centre of the park, to the second crossing. On the right is the Queen Elizabeth Oak, believed to have been planted in the 12th century, which may at one time have been used as a lock-up for park offenders. It collapsed in 1991, after which a new oak was planted beside it by the Duke of Edinburgh. Stately trees are a significant feature of Greenwich Park, and it has many magnificent planes, chestnuts, oaks and alders.

Turn left and go up the slope to a junction with a broad drive. Cross the drive and enter the flower garden through the gate ahead. This is a peaceful haven, shielded from winds by high vegetation all round, with graceful conifers, immaculate flower beds and trim lawns. Follow the path round to the left, then turn right at the end. Walk with rhododendrons and magnolias on your left, and the gardens on your right. Keep to the left until you face a pretty lake, where people like to feed the ducks while pigeons and squirrels clamour for a share.

Walk to the left around the lake, taking a look at the fallow and red deer in an enclosure to your left. Leave the flower garden by a gate and turn right. You are now at the south end of the park and beginning the return route. Walk along an avenue of chestnuts beside the road to a café on the right. Continue past the Planetarium, on which you will see the words Royal Observatory and a bas relief of John Flamsteed. His life is explained in detail in the Old Royal Observatory, which is the next building along and the most popular place in the park.

The Story of Time

If you are at all curious about the modern concept of time, a tour of the observatory is highly recommended. First, you can straddle the Prime Meridian in the courtyard, the point from which the world's longitude and time are measured, then enter Flamsteed House to find out how it all came about. In the first display room are exquisite examples of planispheric astrolabes, which are complex observational and computing instruments used by early astronomers. The next area recounts the frustrating life of Flamsteed, who never solved the puzzle assigned to him by Charles II – to find a reliable method of calculating longitude at sea. Various crackpot methods were proposed before John Harrison came up with a solution that was mechanical rather than astronomical. The problem was that time-keepers of the day were not reliable in rough seas. In the mid-18th century, Harrison devised the prototype time-keeper on which all our modern wrist watches are based. It is interesting to note that Greenwich was designated as the world's Prime Meridian in 1884 – little more than a century ago.

Beside the observatory is the General Wolfe statue, in memory of a local hero who died at the siege of Quebec in 1759, after leading English troops to victory against the French in the struggle for control of Canada. The expansive view from the statue is one of London's best known, taking in most of the park, a long stretch of the river and much of East London. From the observatory, take the steep path down the hill and then branch right along a broad drive that leads directly to the National Maritime Museum.

The Age of Exploration

Just as the observatory tells the story of time as we know it, the National Maritime Museum reveals the history of global exploration by sea. Of course, the two stories were intricately linked; once sea captains could calculate their longitude accurately, they could go where no one had been before. Several of these expeditions ended in disaster, but the golden years of discovery between the 17th and 19th centuries also gave England its greatest exploring heroes – men like Captain James Cook. Other seafaring heroes are also featured, such as Admiral Horatio Nelson, who has an entire gallery of the museum in his honour.

There are over 20 galleries to choose from, and children are sure to enjoy the All Hands gallery, where they can play at loading and unloading ships and being deep-sea divers. However, to take in the whole museum would require a full day. Attached to it is the Queen's House, where you can wander round chambers, apartments and halls once occupied by royalty. The ceiling of the Grand Hall has panels depicting Peace surrounded by the Muses and Liberal Arts, which were originally painted by Orazio and Artemisia Gentileschi, though what you see today are computer-generated reconstructions. One of the nicest touches to the house is the spiral staircase known as the Tulip Stairs.

Through Greenwich Market

Walk westwards along to St Mary's Gate, the main entrance to the park. Turn right to leave the park and walk down King William Walk to Nelson Road. Turn left, noticing the idiosyncratic shops here selling books, antiques and nautical paraphernalia. Cross the road and enter Greenwich Crafts Market, a covered area where more unusual shops compete to catch your attention.

Leave the market by the opposite (north) side, noting the inscription above the exit: 'A false balance is abomination to the Lord but a just weight is his delight.' Cross College Approach, turn right, then left into King William Walk again. Walk past the entrance to the Royal Naval College and the *Cutty Sark* to emerge by Greenwich Pier. After so many walks *beside* the River Thames, there is a unique opportunity here to walk *under* it and view Greenwich from the opposite bank. Just enter the domed building beside the pier, go down in the lift and walk through the cool, damp passage beneath the Thames, to admire the view of Greenwich from Island Gardens.

Option 1 – The Millennium Dome

The Millennium Dome can be reached by strolling 1.5 kilometres (1 mile) downstream along the Thames from Greenwich. Built as the centrepiece of England's celebration of the beginning of the third millennium, it has now joined Big Ben and St Paul's as one of the country's most distinctive landmarks. It is isolated on a peninsula by an enormous curve of the River Thames, and is the world's largest dome with a roof area of 80,000 square metres.

Option 2 – The Thames Barrier

The Thames Path ends at the Thames Barrier, just downstream from Greenwich, so while you are near it is worth taking a look at this phenomenon of engineering (by boat from Greenwich or via the Woolwich Road – A206). Completed in 1984, it is the world's largest removable flood barrier, with gates positioned between concrete pillars that are capped by distinctive stainless-steel cowls. If a surge tide is expected, the gates are rotated from their normal position on the riverbed to stand up and hold back the water. A trip to the visitor centre will explain the complex construction of the barrier, and why it is needed; an experience that will give you a healthy respect for the Thames, which in less than 320 kilometres (200 miles) has grown from a tender trickle to a formidable flow over 500 metres (550 yards) wide. Beyond the Barrier, it is difficult to say exactly where the river ends and the sea begins.

Further Information

Opening Times

There is a charge to enter all attractions listed below unless 'admission free' is stated.

THAMES HEAD

CORINIUM MUSEUM, CIRENCESTER
Open daily except winter Mondays.
April–October: Monday–Saturday
10.00–17.00, Sunday 14.00–17.00
November–March: Tuesday–Saturday
10.00–17.00, Sunday 14.00–17.00
Tel: (01285) 655611
www.cotswold.gov.uk/museum.htm

LECHLADE

BUSCOT PARK
April–September.
House: Wednesday–Friday, second and fourth Saturday and Sunday 14.00–18.00
Garden: Monday–Friday, second and fourth Saturday and Sunday 14.00–18.00
Tel: (01367) 240786
www.buscot-park.com

RADCOT AND KELMSCOT

KELMSCOTT MANOR
April–September on Wednesdays, and the third Saturday in each month in April, May, June and September.
First and third Saturday in July and August 11.00–13.00; 14.00–17.00
Tel: (01367) 252486

NORTHMOOR AND NEWBRIDGE

STANTON HARCOURT MANOR AND GARDENS
Open on alternate Thursdays and Sundays, and Bank Holiday Mondays from April–September, 14.00–18.00
Tel: (01865) 881928

OXFORD

THE OXFORD STORY
April–June; September–October 9.30–17.00
July–August 9.00–18.00
November–March 10.00–16.30
Tel: (01865) 790055
For details of opening times and admission charges of other attractions in Oxford, contact the Oxford Information Centre.

Monday–Saturday 9.30–17.00
Sunday and Bank Holidays in summer
10.00–13.00; 13.30–15.30
Tel: (01865) 726871

ABINGDON

ABINGDON MUSEUM
Summer: Tuesday–Sunday 11.00–17.00
Winter: Tuesday–Sunday 11.00–16.00
Admission free.
Tel: (01235) 523703
ABINGDON ABBEY BUILDINGS
Open summer only, Tuesday–Sunday
14.00–16.00
Tel: (01235) 522711

WALLINGFORD

CASTLE GROUNDS
April–October 10.00–18.00
November–March (weather permitting) 10.00–15.00
WALLINGFORD MUSEUM
Open March–November
Tuesday to Friday, Sunday (June–August) & Bank Holidays 14.00–17.00
Saturdays 10.30–17.00
Tel: (01491) 835065
Cholsey & Wallingford Railway operates short trips with steam trains at weekends in the summer. Call for details
(01491) 835067
PENDON MUSEUM
Saturday, Sundays and Wednesdays during June, July and August 14.00–17.00
Bank Holiday weekends 11.00–17.00
Closed in December.
Pendon Museum Trust. Tel: (01865) 407365

PANGBOURNE

MAPLEDURHAM HOUSE AND WATERMILL
Open Easter–end of September
Weekends and public holidays 14.00–17.30
Tel: (0118) 972 3350
www.mapledurham.co.uk
BEALE PARK
Open 1 March–23 December
10.00–18.00
In winter, the park closes at 17.00 or dusk, whichever is earlier.

Last admission one hour before closing.
Tel: (0118) 984 5172

BASILDON PARK
Open 1 April–1 November
Wednesday–Sunday
House 13.00–17.30
Grounds 12.00–17.30
Tel: (0118) 984 3040

HENLEY
RIVER & ROWING MUSEUM
Monday–Saturday 10.00 Sunday 11.00
Summer closing (April–October) 18.30
Winter closing (November–March) 17.30
Tel: (01491) 415610
www.rrm.co.uk

COOKHAM
STANLEY SPENCER GALLERY
Easter–October, 10.30–17.30 daily.
November–Easter 11.00–17.00 on Saturday,
Sunday and Bank Holidays
Tel: (01628) 520890

CLIVEDEN HOUSE
The gardens are open from March–October
from 11.00–18.00 daily;
November–December 11.00–16.00.
The house (3 rooms only) and Octagon
Temple are open April–October
15.00–18.00 on Thursdays and Sundays.
Tea room open Wednesday–Sunday
11.00–17.00
Tel: (01628) 605069

WINDSOR AND ETON
WINDSOR CASTLE
November–February 9.45–16.15 (last admission 15.00)
March–October 9.45–17.15 (last admission 16.00)
Tel: (01753) 868286
www.royal.gov.uk/palaces/windsor.htm

ETON COLLEGE
Open late March–early October.
Term time 14.00–16.30
Holiday time 10.30–16.30
Guided tours daily: 14.15 and 15.15
Tel: (01753) 671177
www.etoncollege.com

RUNNYMEDE
SAVILL GARDEN
Open daily.
March–October 10.00–18.00

November–February 10.00–16.00
Tel: (01753) 847518
www.savill-garden.co.uk

HAMPTON COURT
HAMPTON COURT PALACE
April–October 9.30–18.00
November–March 9.30–16.30
(Mondays open 10.30)
Tel: (0208) 781 9500
www.hrp.org.uk/index2.htm

RICHMOND
HAM HOUSE
Open end of March–November
House 13.00–17.00
Gardens 10.30–18.00
Tel: (0208) 940 1950

BARNES AND FULHAM
WETLAND CENTRE
Open daily.
Summer 9.30–18.00
Winter 9.30–17.00
Last admission one hour before closing.
Tel: (0208) 409 4400

MUSEUM OF FULHAM PALACE
March–October
Wednesday–Sunday 14.00–17.00
November–February
Thursday–Sunday 13.00–16.00
Tel: (0207) 736 3233

KELMSCOTT HOUSE
Meetings of the William Morris Society
Thursday and Saturday 14.00–17.00
Tel: (0208) 741 3735

CENTRAL LONDON
HOUSES OF PARLIAMENT
The House of Commons Gallery is open
when parliament is in session.
Tel: (0207) 219 3000
www.parliament.uk

FA PREMIER LEAGUE HALL OF FAME
Open daily 10.00–18.00
Tel: (0207) 928 1800
www.hall-of-fame.co.uk

LONDON AQUARIUM
Open daily 10.00–18.00
Tel: (0207) 967 8000
www.londonaquarium.co.uk

BRITISH AIRWAYS LONDON EYE
Open daily.
Phone or check website for opening times.

Tel: (0207) 229 9907
www.ba-londoneye.com
ROYAL FESTIVAL HALL (ALSO QUEEN
ELIZABETH HALL AND PURCELL ROOM)
Call for information about upcoming events.
Tel: (0207) 960 4242
www.sbc.org.uk

HAYWARD GALLERY
Open during exhibitions.
Tuesday and Wednesday 10.00–20.00
Thursday–Monday 10.00–18.00
Tel: (0207) 960 4242
www.sbc.org.uk

NATIONAL FILM THEATRE
Call for information about upcoming films.
Tel: (0207) 928 3232
www.bfi.org.uk

BFI IMAX CINEMA
Call for information about upcoming films.
Tel: (0207) 902 1234
www.bfi.org.uk

ROYAL NATIONAL THEATRE
Daily tours 10.15, 12.30 and 17.30
Tel: (0207) 452 3400
www.nt-online.org

BANKSIDE GALLERY
Open during exhibitions.
Tuesday 10.00–20.00
Wednesday–Friday 10.00–17.00
Saturday and Sunday 13.00–17.00
Closed Monday.
Tel: (0207) 928 7521

TATE MODERN
Sunday–Thursday 10.00–18.00
Friday–Saturday 10.00–22.00
Admission free
Tel: (0207) 887 8008
www.tate.org.uk

GLOBE THEATRE
Exhibition open daily 10.00–17.00
Call for information about upcoming
performances.
Tel: (0207) 902 1500
www.shakespeares-globe.org

VINOPOLIS
Open daily 10.00–17.30
Tel: (0207) 645 3700
www.evinopolis.com

CLINK PRISON MUSEUM
Open daily 10.00–18.00

Tel: (0207) 378 1558
ST PAUL'S CATHEDRAL
Cathedral sightseeing Monday–Saturday
8.30–16.00
Tel: (0207) 236 4128
www.stpauls.london.anglican.org

GREENWICH

CUTTY SARK
Open daily 10.00–17.00
Tel: (0208) 858 3445/6

ROYAL NAVAL COLLEGE
Monday–Saturday 10.00–16.30
Sunday 12.00–16.30
Tel: (0208) 858 2154

OLD ROYAL OBSERVATORY
Open daily 10.00–17.00
Tel: (0208) 858 4422
www.rog.nmm.ac.uk

NATIONAL MARITIME MUSEUM AND
QUEEN'S HOUSE
Open daily 10.00–17.00
Tel: (0208) 858 4422
www.nmm.ac.org.uk

MILLENNIUM DOME
Call 0870 606 2000 to book less than four
days in advance. The Dome is now open
from 09.00–20.00 Sunday–Thursday, and
09.00–23.00 Fridays, Saturdays and Bank holidays. A *Taster Ticket* is available for admission
after 16.00 for late sessions, costing £10 and
giving access to all zones as well as the
Millennium Show and the Blackadder film.
*These Taster Tickets can only be bought on the day,
at the Dome itself.*
www.dome2000.co.uk/tickets

THAMES BARRIER VISITOR CENTRE
Monday–Friday 10.00–17.00
Saturday and Sunday 10.30–17.30
Tel: (0208) 305 4188

Useful Contacts

For information about changes to the path and guided walks:

National Trails Office
Cultural Services
Holton
Oxford OX33 1QQ
Tel: (01865) 810224
Fax: (01865) 810207
www.nationaltrails.gov.uk

For information about path conditions on particular sections:
The Environment Agency
(Flood information)   (0645) 881188
Then dial…   General info 011128
Cricklade - Oxford 011121
Oxford–Marlow 011122
Marlow–Windsor 011123
Windsor–Teddington 011124
London 01111

For information about accommodation and local attractions from Tourist Information Centres:

Cirencester	(01285) 654180
Swindon	(01793) 530328
Faringdon	(01367) 242191
Witney	(01993) 775802
Oxford	(01865) 726871
Abingdon	(01235) 522711
Wallingford	(01491) 826972
Reading	(0118) 9566226
Henley	(01491) 578034
Marlow	(01628) 483597
Maidenhead	(01628) 781110
Windsor	(01753) 743907
Kingston	(0208) 5475592
Richmond	(0208) 9406899
London Tourist Board	(0207) 9322000
Greenwich	(0208) 8586376

Other useful contacts:
The Environment Agency
Tel: (0118) 9355000
www.environment-agency.gov.uk
The River Thames Society
Side House
Middle Assendon
Henley RG9 6AP

The National Trust
(0207) 2229251
www.nationaltrust.org.uk
Ramblers Association
(0207) 3398500
www.ramblers.org.uk

For information about transport services:
Rail operators: (08457) 484950
National Rail: (0345) 484950
www.railtrack.co.uk
Andybus (01666) 505585
Stagecoach (Cirencester)
(01242) 522021
Stagecoach (Swindon) (01793) 522243
Steve's Travel (01865) 883074
Oxford Bus Company (01865) 785400
Stagecoach (Oxford) (01865) 772250
Reading Buses (0118) 8594000

For information about transport in London: (0207) 2221234
www.londontransport.co.uk

For information about boats in London: (0839) 123432

Other boat services:
French Brothers (01753) 851900
www.boat-trips.co.uk
Turk Launches (0208) 5462434
Westminster passenger service
(0207) 9302062
Salter Brothers (01865) 243421

Bibliography

(Books marked ★★ are of particular interest)

Anderson, JRL. **The Upper Thames**. Eyre & Spottiswoode. London. 1970.

★★*Belloc, H.* **The Historic Thames**. Webb & Bower. Exeter. 1988.

Bootle, R & V. **The Story of Cookham**. Cookham. 1990.

Cairns, AJ. **The Book of Marlow**. Barracuda. Chesham. 1976.

Chambers' Biographical Dictionary. Chambers. Edinburgh. 1990.

★★*Chaplin, P.* **The Thames from Source to Tideway**. Whittet. London. 1982.

Collins' Pocket Guide to Wild Flowers of Britain and Northern Europe. Harper & Collins.
London. 1996.

Conduit, B. **Pathfinder Guide to Chilterns and Thames Valley Walks**. Ordnance Survey.
Southampton. 1994.

Conniford, M & S. **To Sonning**. Inkpen. 1981.

Davies, GH. **A Walk along the Thames Path**. Joseph. London. 1989.

De Mare, E. **Time on the Thames**. Architectural Press. London. 1952.

Evans, J. **Marlow through the Ages**. Marlow Tourist Information Centre. 1998.

Fleming J., Honour H. and Pevsner, N. **The Penguin Dictionary of Architecture**. Penguin.
Harmondsworth. 1966.

Gobert, EG. **A Short History of Hurley**. Hurley Preservation Society. Undated.

Handbook Guide to the Thames. Handbook. London. 1998.

Hatts, L. **Walks along the Thames Path**. Patrick Stephens. Wellingborough. 1990.

Hume, IN. **Treasure in the Thames**. Muller. London. 1956.

★★*Jenkins, A.* **The Book of the Thames**. MacMillan. London. 1983.

★★*Joslin, J. and Muldal, A.* **The Thames Path National Trail Companion**. National Trails Office.
Oxford. 1999.

Lawrence, T. **Walks for Motorists: Thames Valley**. Warne. London. 1984.

Lawrence, T. **Exploring the Thames Valley: the Upper Thames**. Countryside. Newbury. 1990.

Livingston, H. **Aerofilms Guide: the Thames Path**. Shepperton. Allen. 1993.

Maple, L. **100 Walks in Oxfordshire and Berkshire**. Crowood. Marlborough. 1997.

Middleton, T. **The Book of Maidenhead**. Barracuda. Chesham. 1975.

Nevell, P. **Rambling for Pleasure along the Thames**. East Berkshire Ramblers. Undated.

Over, L. **The Royal County of Berkshire**. Cliveden Press. Bray. 1995.

Patefield, J. **Thames Valley Teashop Walks**. Countryside. Newbury. 1998.

Perkins, A. **The Book of Sonning**. Barracuda. Chesham. 1977.

Perrot, D. **Ordnance Survey Guide to the River Thames**. Nicholson. London. 1991.

Phillips, G. **Thames Crossings**. David & Charles. Newton Abbot. 1981.

★★*Pritchard, M. and Carpenter, HA.* **Thames Companion**. Oxford Illustrated Press. Oxford. 1975.

Roberts, L. **Pub Walks in the Thames Valley**. Countryside. Newbury. 1993.

Rolt, LTC. **The Thames from Mouth to Source**. Batsford. London. 1951.

Saunders, A. **The Art and Architecture of London**. Phaidon. Oxford. 1984.

★★*Sharp, D.* **The Thames Path National Trail Guide**. Aurum Press. London. 1996.

Index